About David:

David holds a Master of Science Degree in Experimental Metaphysics from Central Washington University. Along with writing, David's career includes being a research scientist in parapsychology, a metaphysical counselor, and a lecturer. David conducts workshops throughout the West Coast on such topics as astrology, tarot, I Ching, healing relationships, and research methodology for metaphysics.

About Lucy:

Lucy's formal education includes a Bachelor of Arts degree in Humanities from the University of Washington. She is a well-known teacher of metaphysics throughout the Northwest and Hawaii, where she operated her own metaphysical center, The Reflecting Pond. In her full-time astrological business Lucy sees clients, teaches classes, lectures, writes, and does taped readings for clients throughout the United States, Europe, Africa, and China. Lucy has served as president and vice-president of the Washington State Astrological Association.

About Jim Sorensen

A Seattle, Washington resident, his formal education in illustration was at the Colorado Institute of Art in Denver. His goal in this book was to bring out the light and fanciful side of metaphysics. He has always had a keen interest in anything unique and fantasy oriented. In fact, he has recently completed a coloring book entitled *The Sons and Daughters of Mystical Creatures*.

THE METAPHYSICAL HANDBOOK

David Pond   Lucy Pond

Illustrated by Jim Sorensen

Reflecting Pond Publications
23 North Orchard Lane
Port Angeles, WA 98362

FIRST PRINTING JULY, 1984
SECOND PRINTING SEPTEMBER, 1984
THIRD PRINTING DECEMBER, 1985
FOURTH PRINTING OCTOBER, 1986
FIFTH PRINTING JULY, 1987
SIXTH PRINTING APRIL, 1988
SEVENTH PRINTING JULY, 1989
EIGHTH PRINTING NOVEMBER, 1990
NINTH PRINTING OCTOBER, 1992
TENTH PRINTING, 1994

Drawings and illustrations ©1984 by Jim Sorensen

Published by Reflecting Pond Publications
23 North Orchard Lane
Port Angeles, WA 98362

ISBN 0-915395-18-5
LIBRARY OF CONGRESS CATALOG CARD NUMBER: 83-091290

Acknowledgements

In offering thanks where thanks are due our deepest gratitude is to life itself. Because of confusing or puzzling situations in which we have found ourselves, and because we want to find answers to the "whys" of life, we have been forced to delve into metaphysics. Here we have been able to unravel and decode some of these perplexing mysteries. Lessons learned through family, friends, and clients have prompted our search. To each of them we are grateful.

There have been numerous key individuals who have directly influenced this book. First we would like to acknowledge Laura Pond, a life mate who has shown how to integrate the teachings of metaphysics into a healthy, happy family. The sacrifice of time and value of her discerning practical wisdom could not be overstated.

Richard Green has influenced this book through his continual belief and support in the nature of our work. He has been a trusting friend of unlimited generosity. Through him, many of our dreams have become reality.

Grace Streitler has had a major impact on this book, not only through her encouragement to stay with it, but also through her deep friendship in times of need. Her insights into the tarot and life itself have provided a constant reminder, confrontation, and affirmation of the reality of the intuitive mind. Joanne Wickenburg has assisted us through the value of her friendship and understanding.

Much of the credit for the actual formation of the book is due to Richard Denner from the Four Winds Bookstore in Ellensburg, Washington. His involvement with research, development, editing, and layout makes him one of the true creators of the book. The diligent and thoughtful editing of Francesca De Capua has earned our appreciation and thanks. She made this book possible for Virgos to enjoy. A thank-you to Barbara Green for her diligent work as our final proofreader.

A very special thank-you goes to Forrest Flashman for his encouragement of this project through the use of his word processor computer.

Finally, we would like to both acknowledge and dedicate this book to our mother. She took on the labor of editing our first draft. Although her red correcting pen often dominated the pages of our original draft, it never masked her love and support. She stayed right with us and eventually there were fewer red marks than copy, and the book was born.

To our Mother, for instilling
the spirit of the quest in us.

CONTENTS

Preface

My involvement with "metaphysics" began long before I had ever heard the term. While growing up I had numerous experiences of a type not talked about at school or in church. During my teenage years I was awakened nearly every night with a sleepwalking experience that sent me off to different corners of the house to let in the souls that I knew were there. Night after night, I would have the same sense: there was a presence that wanted to interact with me. These experiences were not so much frightening as they were disconcerting. In my sleepwalking state, I would try to enlist my family members' help in assisting the trapped souls that I believed were in the refrigerator, the cupboards, the closets, and under the beds. This nightly drama was repeated for years and got to be a family joke. It was not uncommon for me to be standing in my underwear arguing about these matters with whoever was still up. While in the sleep trance, I firmly believed that these presences were there, needing my help. Invariably, I would "wake up" during the conversation with someone laughing at me, and I would go back to bed, embarrassed and confused.

Experiences such as these made my early years tumultuous. No one, outside my family, talked about these types of experiences, so neither did I, for fear of being considered weird. My inner world was confused and, at times, I felt unconnected and isolated from others. When I was nineteen a magical thing happened. My sister, Lucy, who had been studying astrology, prepared my birthchart and interpreted it for me. I was amazed. It was almost as if she had lived my childhood as I did. Even though she was my sister, and obviously had insights into my character from growing up with me, the new information she imparted made me feel she understood what only I had personally experienced. The astrology reading gave me a model for mapping out my inner-world experiences, and this was the first clear connection I had with that realm. I saw in astrology a reference guide for keeping this inner world in perspective.

That first astrology reading, sixteen years ago, sent me off on a search for understanding that has done more for my well-being than any other course of study. I began to wonder if there were other people like me who were having experiences that they felt were unique. By this time, I was a school teacher, and I started asking my second-grade students about their dreams and inner lives. It was soon apparent to me that I was not alone, or even unusual, in my early childhood perceptions. Many children were having inner-world experiences which were not shared with others.

Since my first exposure to metaphysics, I have made the study, application, and use of metaphysical techniques my life's work. I see the oracles as valuable in restoring a sense of meaning to life by providing a structure to organize perceptions and harmonize the inner and outer worlds.

I have been fortunate in being able to work closely with my sister in a continuing effort to bring the metaphysical and occult sciences out from behind the shroud of misunderstanding and confusion and into the clear light of everyday understanding. I am most thankful that we have been there to support each other in work that is not always understood by those around us.

Although two distinctly different individuals, our love of, and belief in, metaphysics is shared to the degree that we can say the writing of this book is "of us." It is our hope that your exposure and involvement with metaphysics will be as enriching for you as it has been for us.

David, 1983
Ellensburg, Washington

The study of metaphysics is a fascinating and seductive endeavor. Once the doors are opened, the techniques and ideas themselves will draw you further and further into the fold. When I was in college studying philosophy, anthropology, and sociology, I didn't come close to grasping even the edge of this world. I had not read even one astrology book and yet I had judged astrology to be simple-minded and somewhat silly. People would ask me, "What is your sign?" They were asking in earnest, but because of my ignorance, I would answer a different sign each time I was asked. To my way of thinking, what difference could it possibly make? If that information was really significant, then they should be able, with time, to figure out that I had lied. But that isn't what happened; they each seemed pleased to discover that I was the sign that I had told them, and it didn't go much deeper than that. Either I was a little like each of the signs, or astrology didn't work at all. In an ironic way, this was my real introduction into the world of metaphysics. It was the time of the Viet Nam War, hippies, political unrest, and mind-expanding drugs. The spiritual search was on.

The theme of the era was "turn on, tune in, drop out." It didn't really matter what you were doing: going to school, being married, holding down a job, being a parent, being a child. Whatever the form your life took, the pressure was on to drop out and find a way to view life from a different perspective. Wasn't this opportunity to stand back from the world and broaden one's perspective the thing that allured people to pot, LSD, and mescaline? Often the very process of trying to find perspective through drugs caused more distortion than what reality itself was offering, but as a general rule, interest and respect was growing for a world that went beyond what was tangible.

Neptune, the planet of illusion/delusion, fantasy, drugs, escapism, spirituality, and supreme faith was in the sign of Scorpio from 1957 until November, 1971. Personal and social values were overturned. Clothes, music, marriage, sexuality, and traditional religion underwent severe transformation. The old ways were no longer in command. Scorpio is the sign of death/rebirth/transformation. It also rules sex. This was the time of free love and peace marches, a search for spiritual meaning rather than material status.

The sciences that are popular in this decade center around computers, quarks, particles, nuclear energy, and metaphysical awareness. There is more going on than meets the eye, and this is continually revealed by the upsurge of popular physics proffered by writers such as Bentov, Capra, and Zukov. The metaphysical nature of energy is raising more and more curiosity. Research is being done on the interfacial relationship between physical reality and mystical reality. Scientists want us to be able to prove what we feel to be true. This may or may not be possible, and even more significantly, it may or may not be imperative to the study and acceptance of metaphysical models.

You are the laboratory where these experiments in consciousness take place. Try the different systems that we present throughout this book. In most cases, you will need nothing more than this book (and an open mind) to allow you to determine for yourself whether the systems work or not.

Lucy, 1983
Seattle, Washington

Introduction

The world around us is always changing. The revolution of scientific information presents a kaleidoscopic panorama, but is it the reality that is changing, or our views of reality? Until recently, science has led us away from a metaphysical approach to life. It had been hoped that the mysteries of life could be solved by an analysis of the physical makeup of reality, yet life is persistently mysterious and magical. The same sciences that directed our view of reality away from metaphysics are once again pointing to a mystical view to explain life.

The term "metaphysics" generates confusion among many. The classical view of metaphysics embraces the ultimate description of reality going beyond the physical characteristics. A popular use of the word "metaphysics" has grown to represent the mystical and occult. This branch of metaphysics embraces the systems that serve as a bridge between the physical reality and the mystical reality. It is this popular branch of metaphysics that we will be dealing with in this book.

There is a transformation of consciousness going on right now that is leaving no aspect of our culture untouched. The old world view from which we are emerging held that the individual was separate from the rest of life. Health researchers now insist all factors of a person's life and environment must be taken into consideration for optimal health. New ideas sprouting from this seedbed have roots in all sectors of our culture and have the dominant theme of "interconnectedness."

It is the scope of our present world problems that is causing such a pervasive response; the world economy, world ecological concerns, and political tensions create the realization that we share a feeling of unrest with all the people of the earth. The current problems affect everyone, so we are at a point where a greater consideration for the individual within the culture is needed.

There are metaphysical techniques which will meet our needs. The study of metaphysics can help us unite with the world and receive relief for the symptoms of alienation. Working with metaphysics can restore the sense of personal meaning which has been lost during this stage of cultural development by providing a framework for actualizing human potential.

The emerging world view of interconnectedness is what this book addresses. All of life is interconnected, and the health and well-being of the individual is a product of the natural flow of communication between all aspects of the whole. Various schools of metaphysical thought (astrology, tarot, I Ching, etc.) are methods for the individual to see how the whole relates to the parts and to organize these perceptions into meaningful concepts. By using the techniques and systems outlined in this book, you will gain first-hand experience of the metaphysical reality.

Each person can be both a receiver and a transmitter of universal knowledge. In the art of divination you seek to align yourself with the clearest channel of information between your essential nature and the wisdom inherent in the universe. The oracular systems presented in this book operate on the premise that there are many aspects of life that are beyond the physical body. The study of metaphysics is the study and synthesis of those aspects of ourselves that go beyond what is physically apparent.

It is now popularly believed that the mind has two halves, each ruling a distinctly different function of the mental process. Most of us have access to both halves, but tend to favor one side. The left brain is said to rule the right side of the body and all thinking that is logical, rational, scientific, and linear. The right brain is said to rule the left side of the body and all thinking that is intuitive, artistic and feeling-oriented. The dominant focus of our culture has been on the advancement of the left side of the brain. This book aims at the integration of the right-brain intuition by using the left-brain techniques presented in the book.

Intuition has many names: insight, E.S.P., luck, and guessing. Although this is a natural function of the human mind, scientists can analyze very little of its operation. Still, intuition is something that most people would admit to having experienced. An example is having a hunch that something will turn out a particular way and then seeing that happen. Another example is thinking about a person you haven't seen or thought of in a long time and then running into that person soon after the thought.

Intuition is often arrived at through random and seldom-understood means. It is accepted, for instance, that games of chance like card gambling and horse racing rely, to a degree, on intuition for success. In these activities, people are seeking riches by attempting to override the rules of logic. In using divination, it is wisdom that is being sought by going beyond what is available through logic. Sadly, we lack training in the proper ways to develop and use this gift. Society places more value on rational, linear thinking than on intuitive insight, so it has not been given the recognition it deserves. This lack of exposure to a natural function has added to the mystery and confusion concerning its use.

Intuition is immediate perception unimpaired by the process of analytical reasoning. An intuitive person understands life's message as one of interconnectedness. Feelings and thoughts must merge for holistic knowledge to be present.

With the study of metaphysics, left-brain techniques and rules are balanced with a belief system embracing right-brain intuition. In using metaphysical tools, we must learn definite rules and techniques before we can simply trust our intuition. Although astrology is called the intuitive science, the intuitive function takes place only after a period of conventional learning. Regardless of how intuitive or perceptive you might be, you will not be a good astrologer until you have learned by rote the fundamental definitions from which the concepts are constructed. Before you start reading the tarot cards, there is much information that must be memorized and assimilated, using the rational left-brain function. Once this has been accomplished, the intuitive right-brain function takes precedence.

Divination is a practice that can help you develop your intuition. Here, you are using the resource of intuition through an active process. The very definition of divination is the process of knowing through the use of intuition. The use of oracles has long been a technique of divination. The oracles provide a structure for the transmission of your intuition. You ask a question of your higher mind and learn to read the response through the oracles. The question is the one variable in the process that you have control over. The more astute you are in asking questions, the clearer your responses will be from the oracles. Much of the art of using the oracles is actually the art of learning how to ask questions. At first, the oracles tend to respond to the unasked question; you may be consciously asking one question but subconsciously asking another. The oracles are uncanny at dealing with the genuine question. With practice, you will learn to ask questions with your whole being, and the responses from the oracles will become more straightforward.

Try the systems. Their worth can not be ascertained by simply observing them objectively; you must get involved with them for their value to be known. The systems are meant to be enjoyed, for they delightfully reveal the full meaning of life's events. These metaphysical systems are stepping stones that can help us cross the barriers of our times while moving toward a new reality.

THE
METAPHYSICAL
HANDBOOK

1

Astrology

My experience with astrology interpretations is that they are typically so well-received by clients that, at times, I've wondered if people will just believe anything, or if astrology can really be that accurate. One situation I was involved with early in my astrology career helped to confirm the accuracy of the birth chart.

When I first met my wife, I drew up her birth chart. The chart showed she had Scorpio rising and when I was interpreting this for her, she said she couldn't accept astrology because her chart just didn't sound like her.

Upon double-checking everything, we found that I had calculated the chart for Seattle when she was actually born in San Diego. With the new information, her chart showed a Libra Ascendant, and the interpretation was received as accurate.

This was the first of a continuous series of affirmations that astrology readings are not general; rather, they are highly specific to the individual.

...David

The model of astrology is one that is uniquely satisfying in the personal search for wholeness. Astrology has the premise that there is a oneness to all of life and that we are all striving for that experience through a multiplicity of ways. Each birth chart represents a unique map of individuality, as well as a connection to the whole of existence. Each planet represents a different area of the total character, and in the quest for wholeness, the more that people know about themselves, the greater the opportunity for creating situations that allow for self-transformation.

Astrology is a technique for understanding change, especially as that change pertains to the process of growth and transformation. The twelve signs of the zodiac are a graphic model of the spirtual awakening process that begins with birth and continues through the course of life. As a model of consciousness, each planet is assigned a symbolic reference to one aspect or layer of consciousness. The ideal is for all the planets to be identified and integrated into the whole of self-actualization and self-exploration.

Astrology is based on the principle of harmony. Watching the heavens, seeing the sun set, the moon rise, and the planets shining, one cannot help but be struck with a sense of beauty, design, and harmony. Simplistically, the intent of the use of astrology is to align personal consciousness with the harmony and order that is present in the heavens. The heavens are always changing but this change is graceful, orderly and harmonious. Change is present in our daily lives as well, but often without the harmony and order of the heavens. The benefit of astrology is that the constant change of planetary configurations provides a model that will help us integrate environmental and personal change into our own lives.

To personalize this model of consciousness, you must have your birth chart calculated. This is accomplished through calculating the positions of the planets at your time and place of birth. These planets are then drawn onto a birth chart that places you in the center of your chart. This becomes a map of the heavens from the perspective of your time and place of birth. No two birth charts are exactly alike, as the heavens move continuously and never repeat any one pattern. These ever-changing patterns afford each of us the opportunity to develop into unique individuals.

The most often-quoted maxim in relation to astrology is "As above, so below." This is the macrocosm/microcosm theory from hermetic philosophy upon which astrology is based. The most common misconception about this relationship between "above" and "below" deals with causality. The doctrine is often interpreted as the planets affecting people's actions. This is a misinterpretation. Astrologers are not assuming that the planets are controlling people any more than they are assuming that people are controlling the planets. What is meant is this: That which is above and below takes part in a larger order — an interconnectedness that is shared by all. There are universal laws of harmony that apply at the human level just as they do at the celestial level.

Astrology has room for free will to operate. By studying your astrology, you can discover what skills, resources, abilities, and opportunities you have been given, but there is no way of knowing through the birth chart which ones of these you have identified and integrated into your life, and which you have left undeveloped. It can show what your major challenges, obstacles, and life lessons are, but does not show which of these you have faced and successfully integrated into your life. Astrology can identify your needs as to relationships, career, and health, but again, there is no way of knowing simply through the birth chart which of these you have acknowledged and identified as your own. Free will is no more taken away from you by astrology than it is if you are given a road map. The choices of destination, routes to take, and how long to spend in an area are choices for you to make; the road map only makes you familiar with the general area. How you personalize your trip is your choice. So it is with astrology.

After you have identified each of the parts of your character that the planets represent, the next step will be to recognize them as cycles. They phase in and out of importance, priority, and ease or difficulty of expression. That is the way of life: a time for everything and everything in its time. These cycles in your life are mirrored by the movement of the planets in their orbits through the zodiac.

When viewed separately, singular events in life appear to be random or even chaotic. It is through seeing these events as parts of greater cycles that they take on a more holistic meaning. Imagine observing the moon only irregularly, and knowing nothing about its pattern of waxing and waning. At times it appears bright and round, at other times we see just a sliver, and at other times it is not visible at all. The unsophisticated mind interprets this as random, but the trained sky-watcher knows that the moon is quite predictable in its pattern of change. Life on earth is a miniature of the cosmic order found in the heavens. It is through watching the patterned regularity of the universe that people are able to interpret the order of human life.

Astrology is the study of cycles. It is the language that connects human life to the universe and then back to the individual. It is a technique of correlating celestial events to behavior in people. One is made aware of the beginning, peak, and end of different types of energy expression. The difference between success and failure is often just a question of timing. Ideas can be good, but if they are not supported by environmental conditions, it will seem impossisble to actualize them. The right time to be aggressive and the right time to be patient with actualization of your ideas is one of the main teachings of astrology. We have all had projects that we have been involved with that have taken all of our energy and more, and still they never get off the ground. At another time, all it takes is to begin and the very same project seems to grow and mature of its own momentum. What makes the difference? Timing.

As you open this door to the vast field of astrology, take the time to analyze the information you are given. Does it work for you? Is it in keeping with what you have experienced in your own life? These questions must be answered by you if this is going to be a meaningful model for you. Once again, you are the laboratory where these experiments in validity are taking place. Be open and critical as you decide whether the information is true or not for you. This whole study is an exciting opportunity to take a closer look at your life and what it means to you.

In its highest form, astrology can help create within you an open attitude toward your individuality and the uniqueness of those around you. Through studying, watching, and being honest with yourself, an atmosphere is created that is similar to psychological analysis. Each of the planets represents one of the particular personality urges for expression, and by studying your birth chart you will be dissecting your personality and seeing how each facet plays its part in your particular path to individuation. Through an in-depth study of astrology, the consciousness is prepared for accelerated growth and development; the extent to which it serves this purpose is the responsibility of each individual who utilizes its techniques.

Astrology is often criticized as being unscientific. It is said its ability to predict events in a person's life is not statistically valid. This point we leave to the scientists to prove or disprove. The scope of our presentation in this book is beyond science. (After all, that is what metaphysics means.) We are offering it as a model of transformation and unification. Astrology serves as an archetype of that process, each sign evolving to the next to incorporate a larger portion of the human experience.

To learn any new language you first must learn its alphabet. With astrology, these will be the symbols that represent the Planets, the Signs, and the meanings of the Houses.

Here is an easy way to remember the role of each of these:

The Planets represent WHAT is going on.
The Signs represent HOW it occurs.
The Houses represent WHERE activity takes place.

PLANETS		SIGNS	
SUN	☉	ARIES	♈
MOON	☽	TAURUS	♉
MERCURY..........	☿	GEMINI	♊
VENUS.............	♀	CANCER	♋
MARS	♂	LEO	♌
JUPITER	♃	VIRGO	♍
SATURN	♄	LIBRA...............	♎
URANUS	♅	SCORPIO	♏
NEPTUNE	♆	SAGITTARIUS	♐
PLUTO	♇	CAPRICORN	♑
		AQUARIUS	♒
		PISCES	♓

Houses

FIRST HOUSE: Persona, physical appearance, beginnings.

SECOND HOUSE: Values, money, and finances.

THIRD HOUSE: Communication, immediate environment, siblings.

FOURTH HOUSE: Home, family, security.

FIFTH HOUSE: Ego, entertainment, enjoyment, children.

SIXTH HOUSE: Work, health, day-to-day routines.

SEVENTH HOUSE: Partners, marriage, reflected self-image.

EIGHTH HOUSE: Taxes, death, transformation.

NINTH HOUSE: Travel, philosophy, higher education.

TENTH HOUSE: Career, profession, public image.

ELEVENTH HOUSE: Group involvements, aspirations, friendship.

TWELFTH HOUSE: Retreat from others, transcendence, limitations.

As you work with the language of astrology it is important to remember that we each have all of the planets, signs, and houses represented in our natal birth charts. They combine differently with each individual, but we each have all of the parts.

The Planets

The planets in astrology represent the various parts of the personality. Each planet plays a necessary and unique role and all of the planets must be operating together to experience integrated wholeness. Planets are found in particular signs based on where and when the individual was born.

Let's use the analogy of the orchestral composer. The planets in their signs are the instruments. The composer must know the capabilities of each of the instruments, and how they sound in various combinations. If you do not know all the instruments and only focus on a few, you can create music, but not to the full potential. If the composer is not aware of the various strengths and weaknesses of the instruments, there is the threat of using them ineffectively, or in clashing combinations. So it is with astrology. By identifying each of the planets and knowing their capabilities, you can orchestrate your involvements with life to make the best use of all your instruments (potentials).

The planets fall into three major groups:

THE PERSONAL PLANETS: Sun, Moon, Mercury, Venus, and Mars. These define the most accessible parts of the personality. They are what distinguish a separate and unique individual.

THE SOCIAL PLANETS: Jupiter and Saturn. These represent the person's connections to the surrounding society; the benefits and responsibilities of being a social creature.

THE TRANSPERSONAL PLANETS: Uranus, Neptune, and Pluto. Beyond the individual and social identity, a person has access to a collective identity. These planets are parts of the character that cannot be controlled, they can only be adapted to. They are beyond conscious control because they operate at a subliminal level.

Each planet can represent a stage in the growth of consciousness, starting from the very self-centered and separate identity which is developed through the Sun, and maturing toward the awakening of a transpersonal identity.

_____⊙_____**THE SUN:** Just as the Sun is the center of our solar system, the Sun in astrology represents the hub of self-identity into which the rest of the planets will integrate. It rules individuality, the drive to BE, the personal will and vitality. Popular astrology, in magazines and newspapers, exclusively deals with Sun-sign astrology, assuming that a person automatically exhibits the characteristics of that sign. Depth astrology, however, sees the Sun as the center of a system, the entirety of which must be integrated for self-actualization to occur. The symbol _____⊙_____ tells the story. An individual comes into life as the dot, with the circle being his or her potential. This is actualized by identifying the other members of the system and harmoniously integrating them into your daily life.

Look to the house of your Sun to see where you are seeking a sense of purpose and meaning in life. Through a prideful involvement with this area of your life, you will feel uplifted and radiant. The sign of your natal Sun shows how to go about achieving this purpose. The activities of the house and the needs of the sign become a focal point in your conscious development as these involvements enhance your sense of vitality.

_____☽_____ **THE MOON:** The Moon represents your response mechanism: how you react to various life situations based on emotional habit patterns. With the Sun as your conscious identity, the Moon is your subconscious, spontaneous response to that identity. The Sun may say what you want to do, but the Moon ultimately allows or does not allow that activity depending on how it FEELS. The Sun and the Moon are an interdependent team.

The Moon describes daily habit patterns, your emotions, and what you need in order to feel at home. At the Sun stage you are working on projecting your identity. At the Moon stage, you don't want to work at any one thing, you just want to retreat into your natural habits, to restore and rebuild, so that once restored, the Sun will be ready to again project into life.

The first balancing and integrating that must take place within the individual is the recognition and identification of these two major themes that are represented by the Sun and Moon. They are harmonized by allowing for equal expression from both. Discord occurs when the individual polarizes to identify with one theme over the other. Then the subdominant theme intrudes and undermines the efforts of the dominant theme. Balance is required.

Look to the house of your natal Moon to see where you emotionally respond to life on a day-to-day basis. Here you are required to be the most adaptable and you are prone to moods of sensitivity due to changes in your environment. This is also the area of life where you retreat when you need emotional rebuilding. The sign of your natal Moon describes how you express yourself emotionally, how you change, and what types of daily involvements you need in order to feel comfortable.

___☿___ **MERCURY:** Mercury is the messenger of the senses. It rules the rational mind and the intellect, and thus, your speaking, writing, and educational preferences. Your ability to learn skills and techniques is also within the domain of Mercury. At this stage, you recognize that you have some control over what you think and what you allow into your mind. You have control over what you pay attention to in life.

By identifying the Mercury function within yourself, you will understand what you tend to gravitate toward in your natural thinking processes. Once you understand this, you have the option to exercise your free will as to whether you will follow your natural tendency or alter it.

Look to the house of your natal Mercury to discover the best learning environment for actualizing mental capabilities. The sign of your natal Mercury describes how your mind naturally operates, communicates, and processes data.

___♀___ **VENUS:** Venus and Mars should ideally be considered together in the model of consciousness. Together they represent the sexuality, drives, desires, pleasures, and values of the individual. Venus is the receptive pole and Mars is the active pole. Venus formulates its values and Mars acts by going out into the world to attempt to bring back the cherished objects. In Jungian terms, Venus represents the *anima* and Mars represents the *animus*.

At the Venus stage of consciousness you become aware of your particular likes and dislikes, which is the beginning of the formation of your personal value system. You begin to know yourself well enough to know that there are certain aspects of life that please you and other aspects of life that displease you. Until you consciously identify these aspects of your personal character, you have no control over them. Your drive for sharing closeness with others is a natural extension of identifying what you enjoy.

Venus represents the pleasure that is available to you when life meets the Venus station needs, but Venus also represents the potential for suffering when these needs are frustrated. At this stage of development you have educated yourself as to your values, what you enjoy most in life, and what you want to share with others. Knowing this, you are better able to educate those closest to you as to how you can be pleased emotionally, physically, mentally, and spiritually.

Look to the house of your natal Venus to see the area of life where you have unspoken needs for appreciation. It is through the areas of this house that you meet and attract potential companions. The sign of your natal Venus describes how you go about attracting love into your life and what types of experiences you most enjoy. The sign also represents the qualities you admire most in others.

____♂____ **MARS:** Mars is the assertive pole of sexuality. It represents how you act out your desires, and how you most comfortably express your animal energy. Sexual drives, frustration, anger, and ambition all relate to this aspect of your character. Before the Mars stage of development, a person is aware of neither what is truly valued, nor how to go out and get it. Frustration is the result, and Mars represents the expression of anger that comes from this.

At this stage of consciousness you begin to know how you spontaneously reach for what you want, and by integrating that with Venus, you will also know if this is in balance with what you value. This gives you the opportunity to exercise free will, and from this point of awareness you can either act on impulse or control the impulse. You know what aspects of your animal nature bring harmony to your total character and what aspects bring dissonance. The choice is yours.

Look to the house of your natal Mars to see where you are most naturally aggressive and exhibit a tendency to be self-assertive. This is the area of life where you are most likely to be passionate and, at times, headstrong. The sign of your natal Mars describes how you go after what you desire.

The planets Sun through Mars are identifiable as personal traits and characteristics. They represent the most malleable and accessible parts of your character.

Jupiter and Saturn represent the social station, where you are given feedback as to how well you have adapted your individuality into society.

_____♃_____ **JUPITER:** How you expand your sphere of influence by taking part in society through philosophy, religion, ethics, and politics is represented by this planet. Before the Jupiter stage of awareness, you are subject to ethnocentricity; believing the philosophy, religion, or political preference that you have been exposed to is the only correct choice, while holding the philosophy and religion of others, who think differently, in contempt. Here you begin to recognize that there are many world views available, each offering its own form of nourishment. Your experience of the world is expanding. Jupiter can also represent the confidence that you feel when you are with others of like mind.

Look to the house of your natal Jupiter to see where you are most optimistic and expansive in your behavior. This is the area where you can be excessive and where you continually require new goals and new food for thought. The sign of your Jupiter describes the type of rewards you are seeking from your social involvement.

_____♄_____ **SATURN:** As Jupiter represents the benefits of being a social person, Saturn represents the responsibility that each person has for maintaining that society. We might say that Jupiter represents the social benefits of having lighted, paved roads, and Saturn represents the taxes you must pay for maintaining those roads.

Saturn represents authority and the laws. Before this stage of consciousness, authority is external, meaning it is something that you have no control over. It lies outside of you, and you can either adapt to it or rebel against it. Here you have the opportunity to internalize authority and take responsibility for your actions. In Jungian terms, Saturn represents the *shadow*, and at this stage you are able to personalize your problems and challenges in society by identifying them as your shadow. Then, instead of seeing the world as unjustly and unfairly imposing restrictions on you, you can see the problems in your life as challenges you have created to integrate a personalized authority within yourself.

Look to the house of your natal Saturn to see where you must overcome limitations and restrictions through realistic and disciplined behavior. The sign of your natal Saturn represents the characteristics of your shadow; the aspects of your life that you are likely to have problems with and project onto others.

The next three planets, Uranus, Neptune, and Pluto, represent energy involved in a transformation process through which you can become more than you were programmed to be through your family upbringing, response to your peers, and community involvement. The energy represented by these planets can be successfully integrated into the personality only after you have met the needs of the preceding planets. The house placement of these outer planets is more important to individuality than the sign, as their orbits are so slow that an entire generation will have the same planet/sign combination.

<u>♅</u> **URANUS:** Uranus represents the voice that awakens the individual to what is beyond personality and social identity. It represents the voice of evolution that enters life unexpectedly and demands attention. Before this stage of consciousness, the ultimate individual is one who is accepted and integrated into the existing society. When things happen that do not fit into the prescribed pattern of conformity, they are considered weird or coincidental, and aren't talked about. To the person who has not awakened to this realm of influence, accidents happen. The lightning bolt of Uranus consciousness zaps the individual's normal world as a reminder of the unexpected in life.

At the Uranus stage of consciousness, there are no accidents. The unexplained is welcomed as evidence that there are events in life over which we have no control. The information coming into conscious awareness via the Uranus function shakes the existing socially-trained structures of your identity. This either evokes fear and resistance in the case of pre-Uranian consciousness, or excitement at the opportunity of seeing life differently at the Uranus stage of consciousness.

Look to the house of your natal Uranus to see in which area of life you seek freedom and independence from the structured way of doing things. This house describes an area of life where you need to express your individuality, where you must deviate from the norm, and experiment with new ways of doing things. The sign of your natal Uranus describes how uniqueness manifests through your generation.

___Ψ___ NEPTUNE: This planet represents your visualization abilities, and the animating force of this vision is imagination. Before the Neptune stage is reached, the individual has no control of this function. Unlicensed, it expresses itself as daydreams, fantasy, escapism through drugs and alcohol, and fanatical beliefs.

Ideally, Neptune represents the stage of consciousness where you identify the imagination process within yourself, and integrate it into your daily life in a healthy manner. Neptune represents the vision that connects you to your transpersonal identity. In esoteric astrology, Neptune represents the umbilical cord between you and God. The power of faith is known to the individual who has integrated this layer of consciousness into his or her being. This is the type of faith that can only be called powerful in its ability to imbue your life with meaning.

Creative visualization, conscious daydreaming, meditation, and prayer are all techniques that can help you in developing this function. Fear, representing the negative pole of the function, responds to this calling from the transpersonal identity with untrusting resistance.

Creativity, whether in art, music, thought, or life style, is the integrated expression of Neptune. Once you have control of your fear and faith, you are not so timid about wandering into the regions of consciousness where creative insights are found.

Look to the house of your natal Neptune to see the area of life where you are extremely sensitive to subtle vibrations. This can either be experienced as confusion and fear, or faith and direction, depending on your ability to control visualization. This is where you can use your mystical imagination to see a better way of life. The sign of your natal Neptune describes the way in which you experience idealism, either in a visionary sense or through delusional forms.

♇ PLUTO: Pluto represents the deepest layers of consciousness and the death and rebirth that must take place to allow for the emergence of your transpersonal identity. This is the area of the subconscious and its contents remain unknown to the conscious side of your being, except through compulsive behavior that is not consciously elicited, revealing hidden motivations. Although this voice cannot be heard consciously, it can be seen through dreams and feedback from others.

At the pre-Pluto stage of development, you do not have access to this layer of consciousness, because you reflect the feedback from others with a simple, "They obviously don't know me." This same dismissal is exercised with dreams, never believing in them enough to allow them into the realm of conscious contemplation. Once you have integrated the Pluto function into your life, this inconsistent feedback concerning self-identity becomes cherished information, pointing to blind spots in your own expression. This can open the door to awareness and ultimate growth as you work with this information.

Look to the house of your natal Pluto to see the area of life where you can learn to read the reaction of other people to see how you can transform yourself into a more conscious person. This is the area where you have the greatest tendency to project your weaknesses onto others and where you have the greatest opportunity to transform yourself by facing your hidden nature. The sign describes an attitude that must be transformed in order to reach a sense of universal selfhood. This sign is also representative of an attitude that your generation has a compulsive need to express.

To get to the transpersonal level you have had to go through the necessary stages of consciousness at the personal and social layers. This forms the solid foundation that is required before exploration of these transpersonal energies is possible. As the total process of growth and expression is accepted and integrated into your life, you have expanded the whole system. Now you are operating in life with a true wholeness.

The Astrological Signs

The first level of awareness concerning the signs is to recognize them as *needs*. Once you have fulfilled the needs of the signs, you are free to use the energy in the way of your choice. The second layer of understanding the signs is through recognizing their potential creative expression. It is important to note that this is not Sun-sign astrology. When we are speaking of Aries, we are not just talking about people whose Sun is in Aries. We each have all of the signs represented somewhere in our charts. Aries is found in each person's chart, along with Taurus, and each of the other signs of the zodiac. As you read about the signs, think about them as attitudes. When you have a planet in a particular sign in your chart, it becomes an emphasized theme in your life. Read each of the signs in terms of their needs and creative expression, and then apply them to your self.

ARIES: _____♈_____ "The Ram;" Ruling Planets: Mars, Pluto

Aries learns through primary experience and involvement with life as opposed to learning from the experience of others. What was true for someone else may or may not be true for the Aries type of individual, and they know it. The need here is to *discover* life and accept its challenges as an adventure.

Aries knows where it is going once it gets there and not before. The best course of direction for Aries to follow is found through listening to their instinctive, gut-level responses to life rather than attempting to follow logical and well-thought-out plans. When they follow their instincts, things work out for them. It is not a good sign for premeditation.

Aries energy is initiating, exuberant, and forceful. Selfhood is defined through the current form of work, activity or creative expression. Action appears to be the answer to all questions.

Aries represents the spring equinox. The days and the nights are now equal, but from this point on, the days will be getting longer. Seeds are being planted for the new year and the plants that survived the winter are again showing signs of life. The long winter's nap is over and animals are coming out of hibernation. Once again the life cycle begins.

CREATIVE EXPRESSION: Once the needs for establishing a self-motivated, independent, and active aspect of life are met, the characteristics of Aries can be expressed in a creative way.

The pioneering spirit belongs to this sign. There is an ability to head out courageously on an adventure, knowing that life will be there waiting to meet those willing to follow their instincts.

Look to the house of Aries in your chart to find where you need to assert your self-identity by trying new experiences. This is the area of life where you have the opportunity to act on impulse and courage. This is a Fire sign, which means that it constantly needs new experiences to serve as fuel for the fire or as a proving-ground for the self. If this testing is not going on, the negative qualities of your Rising Sign or Ascendant are being expressed through your personality. If you are initiating new experiences in this area of life, the positive side of the Rising Sign can be expressed.

Where you have Aries in your chart is the area of life where you bore easily and need feedback from others to develop self-confidence. Here you need to initiate, but not necessarily carry through with activities. This is the area of life where you have difficulty with proper accentuation of what is really important. Watch for selfish, "me-first" tendencies. Aries serves as a spark or catalyst for others and here you can touch people off, bringing out their best and worst.

TAURUS _____ ♉ _____ "The Bull;" Ruling Planet: Venus

The primary need of Taurus is to substantiate experiences generated in your Aries house that you grew to value. In Aries you pioneer new experiences, in Taurus your sense of values is formed so that you grow to appreciate some types of experiences more than others. A sense of self-worth and security is born out of knowing one's skills, resources, and abilities. As an Earth sign, Taurus needs to see tangible results of its actions.

Sensory involvement with life is a must and is aided through affectionate relationships. Taurus is known to thoroughly enjoy touching, holding, and looking at their own highly-valued material possessions. The need for material comfort and security must be met before establishing emotional bonds of security.

The strength of Taurus is found in its enduring value system and the weakness of this sign is the inflexibility of this same system. Because life is a process of continual change, Taurus needs to periodically review its value system as it applies to current situations. Although the need is to establish a meaningful base of operations in the material world, there is a tendency to overdo this. If the investment in the material world is carried too far, Taurus runs the risk of losing its self-identity in the world of things rather than finding it. When this is the case, Taurus manifests itself as greedy, possessive, and inflexible.

The energy of Taurus is gathering, collecting and consolidating. Taurus occurs at the height of spring. Leaves are now on the branches and many of the buds forced in Aries have begun to produce flowers. Root systems are forming underground to insure that the seedlings will endure. Mating is occuring in the animal world.

CREATIVE EXPRESSION: Once the primary need of material security and awareness of personal values is met in Taurus, its creative expression can be experienced. The cultivation of the enjoyment of the senses can be refined to make Taurus a real connoisseur of life. Taurus is here to show us that this life, in the here and now, is available for enjoyment. The Taurus appreciation of beauty is found in a wide variety of forms that titillate the senses.

For Taurus, consciousness, growth, and spirituality will be found through experiences in the material world rather than renunciation of it. The need is to integrate spiritual identity into the material world.

Where Taurus is located in your birth chart is where you must define what is personally important to give you a sense of rootedness. Be careful not to get lulled into accepting society's symbols of success without personal consideration. Taurus is where you have an innate common sense that is intimately tied to your value system, letting you know what is best for you. Trust this.

In its highest form, Taurus represents rapport with nature: planets, rivers, trees, and sunsets. Taurus can be restored and revitalized through time spent outdoors in nature. (They really do like the smell of freshly cut grass.)

Look to Taurus in your chart to see where you find security through a sense of rootedness, routine, and predictability. This house represents an area of life where you need tangible results. Abstracts, potentials, what should be, could be, might be....will not work for you here; what IS is what matters to you. This is also an area of life where you can be stubborn and inflexible.

GEMINI: ___Ⅱ___ "The Twins;" Ruling Planet: Mercury

In Gemini the primary need is to establish connections with the surrounding environment. Intellectual awareness is born as a spurring-on of the search for mental stimulation. This leads to the development of communication skills as the tools of the trade to fuel the Gemini need for data and information.

Immensely curious, there is a childlike wonder and fascination with the world. "Variety is the spice of life" was surely written with Gemini in mind. Their communication skills and wide-ranging interests make Gemini types lively conversationalists with quick and witty minds.

This same hunger for variety can lead to a superficiality, leaving the Gemini unreliable, fickle, and flighty. Geminis are genuinely interested in how the threads of connection intertwine through people. This is extended to the love of all types of media and communication particularly if it is directed toward them. Geminis are accused of signing up for junk mail! They are curious about resources they may never use. If you want to know where you can buy a solar-powered blender, ask a Gemini. He probably doesn't have one, but he just read something about them in one of his periodicals, and still has the article that you can borrow.

In the cycle of the seasons, the leaves and flowers are now in full bloom as Gemini represents the final stage of spring. The night force is waning and the days continue to grow. The air feels full of life and there is an urge to experience the wonder of it all. Gemini marks a transition from the last stage of spring into summer.

CREATIVE EXPRESSION: The childlike curiosity of Gemini can make this the least judgmental of the signs. Everything that comes up to be considered is evaluated in terms of just that particular moment. Geminis' interest in a wide variety of communication leads them to be the integrating links between divergent sources of information. This can make them the synthesizers of the idea world. The search for mental stimulation brings the Gemini face-to-face with the world of computers, electronics, puzzles, games, and words. It can even lure them into creating mental puzzles out of their lives.

The creative expression of Gemini is pure mental gymnastics expressed in a variety of forms; linguistics, writing, speaking, research, and teaching, to name a few. Any arena that includes the flow of information is home court for Geminis and gives them the best opportunity to shine.

Look to the house of Gemini in your birth chart to see where a non-judgmental attitude is required to experience variety and a sense of wonder about life. This is the area where you are open to experiment, and where you have a tendency to scatter your energy. This is where you can be accused of being fickle because your interest changes often.

With Gemini, the license of curiosity is given to explore life, but this curiosity can change into indulgence if you are not applying and integrating all that you have learned.

CANCER: _____⌀_____ "The Crab;" Ruling Planet: The Moon

The reaching out in Gemini is consolidated in Cancer with the need to establish boundaries. At this stage, it is the depth of experience that is significant rather than the breadth that was prevalent in Gemini. The first need of this sign is to establish emotional security. After this has been defined, the second part of the process begins; the need to be involved in a nurturing relationship with someone or something. The sense of belonging is of ultimate importance to Cancer, leading them to a rich family life, parenting and social attachments. Their role in society is not that of a reformist but that of a conformist.

With so much concern over boundaries and emotional attachments, there is a natural resistance to new experiences and people that must be overcome. This leads to two types of Cancer expression.

If you are at the stage of formulating your territory, you are expressing the "Sentinel" type of energy. This is typified by a patrolling and protecting of boundaries, always watchful of potential danger. Cancer is ruled by the crab, an animal with a hard outer shell that protects the vulnerable and soft inside. Cancers will not face confrontation head-on but rather, like the crab, move sideways to avoid anything that might jeopardize their emotional security. This symbol is most fitting of this stage of expression.

Once the boundaries have been defined and there is comfort concerning basic security needs, the "Nurturer" is allowed expression. This type exhibits the true strength of Cancer, and if you are lucky enough to be in their inner circle, you'll feel cared for, loved, and protected. The Nurturer's most natural role is parenting. This energy is expressed through the home, domestic life and their family of friends.

Cancer is the time of year of the summer solstice, the longest day and the shortest night. At this point of the yearly cycle the days will begin to shorten and the nights will grow longer. This shift causes the remembrance of past winters and the realization that one must once again work on establishing a secure home and foundation if one is to be prepared for the future.

CREATIVE EXPRESSION: Cancer rules the urge to seek one's place in the universe by defining boundaries, borders, and anything that will help substantiate one's security. It rules the urge to have a private and secure place away from the clamor of the world. This is an emotionally deep sign that is sensitive to all surrounding vibrations. Cancer is here to teach us that it is safe and healthy to feel emotions.

Look to the house of Cancer in your birth chart to see where you need clearly defined boundaries in your life. This is where you seek nourishment through establishing emotional bonds of security. This is also an area where you can be overly sentimental and allow your attachments to the past to block you from new experiences.

LEO: _____ ♌ _____ "The Lion;" Ruling Planet: The Sun

In Leo there is an urge to express all that was stored and nurtured in Cancer. The ego is born as the desire to see itself reflected through forms of creative self-expression. Like its planetary ruler, the Sun, the will to be the center of attention is balanced with a desire to grace its audience with affectionate warmth. For this to occur there are three needs that must be met: 1. They must be in heartful relationships. 2. They must be the center of attention in some area of life. 3. They must be having fun in their lives. When any one of these three needs are not met, the warm, affectionate Leo cannot surface. Instead, they appear stubborn, selfish, and arrogant. It is ultimately Leo's responsibility to find the proper types of relationships and life situations that allow for these needs to be met.

In the seasons, Leo represents the hottest time of the year when all the fruit is maturing to the ripest stage just prior to being picked. Because of the intensity of the heat, this is the time of year to pull back from a heavy work routine. It is time to relax and enjoy life.

CREATIVE EXPRESSION: Once the Leo needs are met, this sign can emanate the qualities of a powerful, fun, and creative life. The gift of joyousness is available to Leos if they search in their hearts. Joyousness is a product of a person doing what he really enjoys. Imagine the following test: there is a grocery store with ten food checkers. Of the ten, only one of them really enjoys the job. You have fifteen seconds to identify that one person. Would you be successful? Most likely, yes, because that quality of joyousness would be evident.

Leo is here to teach us about the love of life that comes from following the heart. The power of love does assure Leo success in life. A basic question for Leos to consider is whether it is the love of power, or the power of love that is motivating them. Any of the creative arts or business can provide the challenge and opportunity to shine that Leo has to offer.

Where Leo is in your birthchart is where you dramatically express your individuality, creativity and generosity. It is here that you seek approval from others. This house can also represent an area of exaggerated self-importance that can lead to arrogance and selfishness. Here you need to shine and be the center of attention.

VIRGO: _____ ♍ _____ "The Virgin;" Ruling Planet: Mercury

In Virgo, the urge to perfect and refine the creative expression of Leo becomes a driving force. Energy is organized into techniques and systems of expression. Virgo is characterized by three primary needs, which are analyzation, discrimination, and integration. These are the steps that Virgo takes to digest life experiences. As the perfectionist, Virgo is inherently aware of each flaw in personal performance and there is a consistent drive to improve upon existing conditions.

Virgo is the last of the personal signs and it is here that one becomes aware of the fine adjustments in self that are necessary before entering the social arena.

This is the time of the harvest; all of the fruit is mature and ready to be picked. The symbol of Virgo is the Virgin; a beautiful and seductive woman ready to share her essence in the act of creation. When the timing is right, Virgo is one of the most sensual signs of the zodiac.

CREATIVE EXPRESSION: Once the self-analysis of Virgos is balanced with an equal measure of self-acceptance, their qualities find plenty of room for expression. Virgos are really team players; they do not need to be in the limelight as long as their contribution is appreciated. Virgo is the voice of efficiency and effectiveness, and Virgos apply themselves to tasks with this attitude. Anything that takes an eye for detail and the application of technique is the natural domain of Virgo. This is the sign of the craftsperson who can take a skill and polish it to perfection. "The earth belongs to those who take care of it" was probably written about Virgos. Their ability to care for and maintain that which they have usually keeps Virgo's world highly tuned. Combine this with their desire to be of service and it shows that Virgos can be wonderful health educators.

Look to Virgo in your birth chart to define the area of your life where detail work is required and where maintenance and efficiency are required to feel progress. This is where you need to set REALISTIC standards, as some self-acceptance is needed to balance the discrimination.

LIBRA: _____ ♎ _____ "The Scales;" Ruling Planet: Venus

At this stage of growth, learning takes place through seeing how one relates to others. Social consciousness is born with the emergence of the comparative self. Cooperation is now required to reach goals. Here it becomes important to listen to what others are saying, as one learns through sharing and interaction.

The Scales, the only inanimate symbol of the zodiac, represents the sign of Libra. Librans can be cold in their analysis of justice and fairness. They rule the legal system as well as armies and war. This is the sign that is willing to fight for what is right.

Whether it is the clothing, home environment, or dinner, Librans want it to look and feel a certain way. They can add beauty and grace to all of their involvements. This sense of design works well with art and music, and is difficult to integrate into attitudes about relationships. They want relationships to be flowing, and always without problems. They know how it should be and how they want it to be, having a tendency to relate more to the IMAGE of the relationship than the actual person involved. This is a sign that can be found going from one extreme to another seeking balance and harmony in life.

Libra is the time of the autumnal equinox. The day and night forces are equal, and from this point on the night force will continue to grow past the day force. Nature is beginning to slow down and the color of the leaves is changing from green to orange and red. People also begin to slow down, spending more time indoors, cultivating their inner worlds and social relationships.

CREATIVE EXPRESSION: When the personal self and the social self are balanced, the eloquence, beauty, and grace of this sign is naturally expressed. As an Air sign, Libra is mental in its approach to life. The artistic and literary fields offer the best opportunities for these types. Justice, fairness, and equality are all important to Librans, giving them natural abilities in all of the legal professions. The fashion and beauty industry, as well as interior design, can also prove to be satisfying for the expression of their refined natures.

Look to Libra in your birth chart to see where you need support and feedback from others. This is where cooperation will work more effectively than initiation; where listening is more important than speaking. This house also represents an area where you can lose your personal identity through becoming more and more dependent upon others.

SCORPIO: _____ ♏ _____ "The Scorpion;" Ruling Planet: Pluto/ Mars

In Libra, one forms relationships with others. In Scorpio, one allows one's self to be psychologically affected by the other person. The process of transformation begins as one creates bonds of heart and spirit with another person.

The types of personalities manifested through Scorpio are as different as the types of animals used as its symbols. If the self is not willing to face its own hidden nature, there is the Scorpion: guarded, defensive, and intuitively aware of the weaknesses of others; wanting to sting and frighten potential loved ones before there is a chance of being hurt. If the self is willing to confront its own hidden nature, there is the Phoenix, the mythological bird which rises out of the fires of the death of the old self. Finally, there is the Eagle that sees where problems, both real and potential, lie, and chooses to fly above them.

On the lowest level, which must be passed through to get to the higher levels, there is revenge, resentment, and holding on to past pains. It is not that they enjoy revelling in the past; there is a genuine intent to get to the bottom of a problem before moving on. The question is, when do you ever reach the bottom?

There is an appropriate analogy with a dark room. The Scorpio walks in and sees that it is dark, and wants to get rid of the darkness. The focus is on the darkness. He takes a shovel and starts digging out the darkness, shovel by shovel, scooping out the darkness with more and more intent, sincerity, and passion. However, the room remains dark. Later, a friend comes over and says, "Hey, it's dark in here!" and turns on the light. The lesson to learn is that you can't get rid of darkness by focusing on it. You must go beyond and above the situations of pain and darkness, which are the lessons of the Phoenix and Eagle.

There is a fear of being paralyzed by their emotions, which Scorpios can view as a tidal wave. This belief leaves them cautious and protective of what, or whom, they allow their emotions to merge with. They have the capacity to be intensely molded by emotional involvement and they cautiously manipulate, or even avoid this area of life.

This sign needs intrigue and intensity, making them absolutely fearless about taboos. This same interest can also lead to entanglements concerning attitudes about sexuality, possessiveness, jealousy, money, and death.

The signals in nature point to an inward turning of the life force, leading to a more psychological effect of transformation. The bright colors of Libra are now changing to browns as the leaves begin dropping from the trees. Life in the plant kingdom is becoming less apparent as life moves beneath the ground for the remainder of the winter months. Dead leaves are being used as the fertilizers for the ground. People begin spending more time indoors as the nights continue to grow and the days are getting shorter.

CREATIVE EXPRESSION: Once desire is curbed and directed into healthy channels, the creative gift of the ability to transform is available. Scorpio is ultimately concerned with merging and transforming. This makes Scorpio the sign of the alchemist who can take raw human emotions and transform them into golden potential. Scorpio is sensitive to the intentions and motivations of others which makes them very effective healers. The healing professions, the literary fields, and all matters of investment and financing make use of Scorpio's abilities.

Look to the house of Scorpio in your birth chart to see where you desire to control situations and need to allow for the transformation that comes through surrendering. You approach this area of life with passion and intensity, and it is here you must be willing to analyze your motivations. There is a tendency to be secretive concerning the matters of this house.

SAGITTARIUS ___✗___ "The Archer;" Ruling Planet: Jupiter

In Sagittarius, there is an urge to expand out of the emotional limits of Scorpio, to get out of the intensity and entanglements, and see the world. The Archer is seeking enthusiastically to expand the boundaries of thought, religion, and philosophy. Another symbol for Sagittarius is the Centaur, half horse and half human: dualistic in nature. The first side is physical sports and action-minded, with the urge to explore the capabilities of the body through competition. The other half of the body is also strong, but on a philosophical, mental, and idealistic level. There is often a battle raging within the Sagittarian between the esthetic and refined versus the physical, passionate and sensual side of one's nature. Is the horse carrying the person, placing the horse in control, or is the person riding a horse? This is a question that, until answered by Sagittarians, keeps them tripping over the earth because their heads are off in the clouds. The lesson is to incorporate the two into equal and balanced expression.

Here are the dragon-slayers. They always need a major goal in front of them (preferably, one that is impossible to reach). The tendency is to have too many of these going at once, which can make the Sagittarian scattered and superficial.

The Sagittarian is a truth-seeker, and as all Fire signs, very idealistic. This idealism fuels their optimism and enthusiasm which typically makes them jovial, outgoing and fun to spend time with. Strong quest for adventure is present, with a tendency to overdo out of extreme optimism. Keen awareness of future potentials is a Sagittarian trait with the potential itself often being its own reward. "I could do that if I really wanted to," is an attitude that can keep them from actualizing these challenges. Sagittarians tend to be dogmatic in their moral and ethical stances, which leads to a tendency toward proselytizing because of extreme eagerness to share the "good news" of the new "truth" they have found. Sagittarians like to focus on the large picture, often ignoring the details along the way.

This is the time to share the year's harvest with others. Thanksgiving is celebrated, which is a time of merry-making, eating and drinking. It is a time of giving thanks and reaping the rewards of the year's efforts.

CREATIVE EXPRESSION: Once harnessed, the adventurous spirit of Sagittarius can send these people far and wide, both in physical and mental travel. A penchant for words and philosophy, coupled with their experiences in travel, make them effective at expanding the world view of the people they contact. As the last of the Fire signs, Sagittarius represents sustained fire. This gives them an air of confidence that can be both inspiring and motivating to others. Sagittarians are born teachers, so any field that allows them to share or gather information is a natural for these people.

Look to your house with Sagittarius on it to see which area in life you can approach with confidence and optimism to go beyond your present boundaries of experience. This is the area of life where your eagerness for the breadth of experience keeps you from total commitment to any one form of expression. The Archer needs a target and so it is here that you will need clearly defined goals to focus your enthusiasm. Look for resources beyond your immediate environment for opportunities concerning this house.

CAPRICORN: ____ ♑ ____ "The Goat;" Ruling Planet: Saturn

The over-extended boundaries of Sagittarius are brought into manageable limits with Capricorn. Organization of resources is of paramount importance as one becomes motivated to create a socially respected role. The philosophies, morals, and laws that were talked about in Sagittarius are brought into form and enforced in Capricorn. Social power, authority, and above all, respect are the goals of this final Earth sign.

Capricorns are elitists who can do well within any system. They have an intuitive feeling for the significance of rules and are willing to follow them. They appreciate organization and operate well within it. This attitude allows them to reap the rewards of society.

The key phrase for the sign is "I Use." Although accused of using people, it would be more accurate to say they are resourceful, knowing the best use of people and materials they come in contact with. Capricorns need large basements to house all the stuff they gather along the way. Walking down the street one might see a spring and say, "This ballpoint pen spring is something I can use for my carburetor." They are good at improvisational USE of things, knowing what fits, where, and how. If you ever need a special size nut or bolt, go to the Capricorn's house; they are likely to have it in their basement.

The dire side of Capricorn comes through when they take their responsibilities too seriously. Forgetting to put FUN on the schedule of valuable things to do with one's time can be a problem. Capricorn can also be over-cautious in all dealings with the heart. They can appear to be cold and calculating but it is often insecurity that stands in the way of their expressing warmth. Developing friendship with a Capricorn happens in steps, as you must earn their trust before they will totally open up. Loyalty and commitment are important to this sign.

At this part of the cycle in the seasons, most of the plant life is dormant. The winter solstice occurs, which is the time of the longest night and the shortest day. Religious holidays are celebrated to focus on the light of faith at this, the darkest time of the year.

CREATIVE EXPRESSION: The goal-oriented, serious, and ambitious approach to life gives Capricorn strong social responsibility and managerial skills. These traits show through both on the job and in a general aptitude for pin-pointing what people would be good at. They know what their social station needs to be for them to feel comfortable, and they can appear restless in social situations until these goals are met. It will probably take years, maybe even the whole first half of life, but once that has been accomplished, they allow themselves to relax and enjoy life. At this point, they start to grow younger.

As the last of the Earth signs, Capricorn represents practical wisdom. Capricorns can become the pillar of strength for people in their lives because of the father image they project.

Look to your house with Capricorn on it to see where you must work until you have achieved your desired goals. Develop a managerial attitude toward the matters of this house to achieve success. This is the area in life where you crave social approval and where clinging to established ways can cause a rigid presentation of self. This is an area where you need to build form and structure in your life by facing matters realistically. Time is on your side with Capricorn, and here you need to plan for the long road ahead.

AQUARIUS: _____♒_____ "The Water Bearer;" Ruling Planet: Uranus.

After the established, routine-imbued structure of Capricorn, Aquarius comes in as a reminder that it is possible to move beyond social boundaries and express personal uniqueness. There is a rebellious spirit against any form of restraint. The awareness moves from collective rights to individual rights. There is a desire to reform structures so they continually evolve to the ever-changing needs of humanity. An attitude of "fight against the system if it is not allowing you to do what you want" is born with this sign. Aquarians need a sense of purpose and direction to channel their energies or they will develop wanton rebelliousness.

Aquarians must believe in their uniqueness and originality in order to express it. These are the non-conformists who find following "herd consciousness" suffocating. Emotional and sentimental expression can also be suffocating, as the need for freedom propels Aquarians away from emotional involvements.

As the last of the Air signs, Aquarius represents abstract mental abilities. The quest is to fit everything into a universal perspective. Their tendency toward intellectualization makes them appear aloof and unreachable in regard to personal concerns. When confronted on this issue, an Aquarian might respond by saying, "It's just that your personal problems seem so insignificant compared to the problems of the world."

Unconventionality is important to the degree that Aquarians will often go to great lengths to be different from others. Aquarians need to learn that it isn't necessary to fight for something already have. Their revolutionary spirit can send them fighting for the independence, freedom, and uniqueness they were given at birth. They need to recognize and exercise these qualities within themselves before they ask others to recognize them.

In this late winter sign the nights are still the longest but the days are increasing in length, encouraging hope for the future that Aquarians are known for. Spring will come; however, it is still winter and the time is for planning, dreaming, and scheming, rather than action. Sharing ideas with others is an activity that is favored at this time.

CREATIVE EXPRESSION: Aquarius is here to remind us of the

individual (all individuals) within society. They represent the evolutionary voice of culture, drawing attention to those aspects of society that need to be reformed. As evolutionary agents, the vision they hold is often shocking to others. They must learn to accept this. It is good to make people think.

The eccentric lifestyle and unconventionality of Aquarians affords them a unique perspective on society that would otherwise go unnoticed. For this view to be accepted, Aquarians must take responsibility for their visions. By seeing what is lacking in society, they are really seeing their own job description.

Look to the house of Aquarius in your birth chart to see where you are seeking freedom from old, established ways of doing things. Here you can trust your uniqueness and inventiveness, rather than convention, for success. This is the house where you have an intuitive sense about the future, and it can also be where you exhibit a "know-it-all" attitude. In your search for clarity in the activities of this house, you may have developed an aloofness that makes you seem unapproachable.

PISCES: _____ℋ_____ "The Fishes;" Ruling Planet: Neptune

As the final sign of the zodiac, Pisces represents an accumulation of all the previous signs. The boundaries that separate one from another are dissolved with the Pisces sensitivity that feels beyond boundaries. The need is to understand and unify all experiences with an all-encompassing faith. There is a tendency to side with the underdog which can lead to a martyr-type approach to life. Pisces is the most sensitive of the signs, as is demonstrated by the fact that they are sometimes overwhelmed by the world. When this is the case, they need some sort of escape or fantasy as a retreat from their intense feelings.

The two fish of the Pisces symbol reflect the sign's inherent duality that must be brought into balance. One fish is swimming in the waters of earth, and the other in the waters of heaven. Pisces can appear to be other-worldly or "spaced out" when they exhibit this ethereal part of their character. Conversely, an over-focusing on the pleasures and comforts of earthly life can lead to the exclusion of the spiritual life. Ideally, the spiritual and earthly sides of the character are balanced so that Pisces can direct their worldly affairs of daily involvement with an integrated faith. The inner world of emotions, feelings, thoughts, and fantasies is just as important to Pisces as the outer world of events. Because of this, they need a certain amount of time by themselves daily.

Pisces needs to *feel*; if they can feel good, fine, but if not, they would rather experience pain than no feeling at all! Pisces must take responsibility for the way they feel in this life, and ask themselves the question, "Do I feel the way I do because of the events that have happened to me, or have the events happened because of the way that I feel?"

The Pisces need for inner-world experiences is generated from a very active imagination. This imagination is a resource for Pisces that they cannot afford to waste. Imagination fuels both fear and faith and this duality is presented to Pisces as a choice. If they do not make a conscious choice, they are subject to the emotional currents around them. Without direction, the imagination functions through fantasy, illusion, escapism, and daydreaming. With direction and the cultivation of faith, this same imagination gives creative visualization skills in art, music, and spirituality.

Pisces is here to accept everyone and everything, including themselves. A tendency to neglect the care of their own souls often leads them to martyring roles. Pisces can be prodded into emotional relationships through pity. In a situation where Pisces find themselves sacrificing their personal happiness, they should evaluate their motivations.

As the last of the winter signs, Pisces is the time when the previous year's cycle exists in memory and feeling. With spring and new activity just around the corner, this is the time to absorb the meaning of the cycle just ending.

CREATIVE EXPRESSION: Once the sensitivity and imagination is brought under control in Pisces, they can develop a powerful faith that can imbue their lives with meaning. Pisceans see how it all fits together, and they can be called on by others as counselors and listeners. When Pisces have elevated the soul in their lives, they become a model for all humanity of how to integrate the etheric and earthly aspects of character. Pisces is here to be a living symbol of the power of faith.

Look to Pisces in your birth chart to see where you are seeking to dissolve barriers that separate you from others. You may experience accute emotional sensitivity concerning the matters of this house. Faith and acceptance must be cultivated in this area of life to provide shelter for sensitivity, or escapist tendencies may emerge.

The Houses

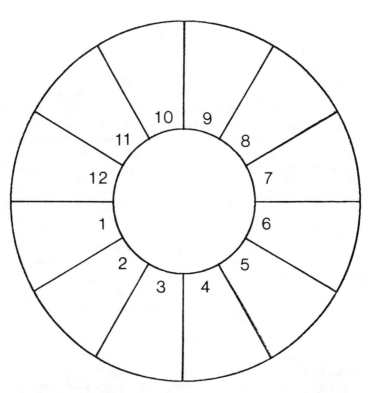

There are twelve houses in a birth chart, each one describing an area of life where activity takes place. The first house is in the same position in every birth chart (beginning at the equivalent of nine o'clock on the face of a clock), and the houses progress counter-clockwise from there. The sign on the *cusp* (line separating one house from another), and the planets falling within each house, indicate how a person goes about meeting the needs of the house. As you develop the qualities of this sign, the environment opens up the activities of the house in a most natural way.

As you read through this section on the houses, be aware of it as a total process of integration. Notice how the energy in one house sets up the prerequisite for learning and the lessons to be learned in the next. Look to your birth chart and notice where you have clusters of planets. Where you have planets located is where you attract concentrated experiences from life.

The first house is a house of initiation, and the second house is a house of consolidation. The combination of these form the rhythm of astrology. All of the houses follow this pattern.

INITIATION: All odd-numbered houses: 1,3,5,7,9,11

CONSOLIDATION: All even-numbered houses: 2,4,6,8,10,12

FIRST HOUSE: The first house and its beginning point, the Ascendant (also called "Rising Sign"), represent the primal drive to establish oneself as an independent identity. From the twelfth house of the universal and collective, the first house emerges like an individual raindrop emerges from the cloud; like millions of other raindrops, yet individual with distinctive characteristics and boundaries. The compulsion "to be" is the compelling drive that leads one to pose the question "Who am I?"

The sign located on the cusp describes how you initiate new activities, and it describes the qualities of your persona or mask that you "put on" to deal with the world. The Ascendant is a door-opener to the environment. If you develop the qualities of your Rising Sign and integrate these qualities into the projection of your personality, your environment will be more responsive to you.

SECOND HOUSE: The consolidation of self begins by a process of self-awareness through developing and sorting out personal likes and dislikes. You become aware of who you are by what you value and what you appreciate. You begin developing comfortable surroundings, and you add sustenance to your being by attaching yourself to objects that reflect who you are.

The sign on the cusp of your second house describes how you go about getting in touch with the skills, resources, and abilities that are the tools of your personal self-security. It also describes your attitudes about the material world, money, and finances.

THIRD HOUSE: Here begins the process of recognizing the interrelatedness of you and your environment. Communication skills are developed to form connection between you and others. This is the area of the rational, logical mind and this is the house that rules speaking, letter-writing, phone calls, and conversation. Curiosity and wonder are born. How and why things work are of interest.

The sign on your third house cusp describes how you approach your environment, your relatives, and siblings. It also describes the nature of your curiosity toward the unknown, and how you tend to communicate your thoughts.

FOURTH HOUSE: Here is where self-identity is consolidated. The process that started with an instinctive drive for expression in the first house, a formation of values in the second house, and an awareness of the environment in the third, completes itself in the fourth house. Boundaries based on personal experiences are set and within these you are comfortable expressing the real you. Memory along with emotions are born in this house. Home and family become recognizable symbols of comfort and security.

This is the midnight point of the chart, and is considered the point of deepest psychological confrontation with the self. The sign on your fourth house cusp describes how you go about the process of feeling psychologically secure with yourself. It also describes the qualities of your self-image, and the type of home environment you can set up.

FIFTH HOUSE: Here is where you need to dedicate your newly-formed identity to a sense of purpose that is linked with the creative expression of your skills and talents. The offspring of your creative identity, be it love affairs, drama, music, or children is a "putting to use" of the energy that comes from knowing yourself. Here is where the will is formed and used, and the ego is created. This is the house of creative self-expression, romance, and entertainment.

The sign on your fifth house cusp describes your attitude concerning your creative abilities and your ability to assertively express yourself. How you approach pleasurable activities is also indicated by this sign.

SIXTH HOUSE: This house represents the final consolidation of the subjective experience of life; the process of discrimination. The mind becomes analytical in the process of self-examination. Here you become aware of the self-adjustment that must occur before becoming an effective participant in social relationships, which is the activity that follows this house.

How you develop daily routines to help develop optimal health and overall effectiveness in life are described here. These can take the form of exercise, diet, schedules, lists, and attitudes toward your work. The sign on your sixth house cusp describes how you make personal adjustment and describes your techniques of self-improvement. It also describes your attitudes toward creating a healthy work environment.

SEVENTH HOUSE: In the seventh house there is awareness of others and the birth of objectivity. Cooperation and relating become important aspects of the personality. This is where you can complete your personal image by including the reflected image, or shadow, cast by the response from others to your actions. A relative image develops through awareness of those whom you attract.

The sign on your seventh house cusp describes the partner you need for the clearest reflection of yourself. It also describes attitudes toward others. This sign represents qualities you can develop to open the door to relationships.

EIGHTH HOUSE: The eighth house is a consolidation of the seventh house explosion into the world of others. This house represents a confrontation with the self. Here one sorts out the seventh house experiences, separating the most valuable and meaningful from the others. Awareness of personal limits leads to identification with symbols larger than self, such as business, money, power, and sex. Here you will be confronted with deep-rooted patterns of control and security, shown through compulsive or addictive patterns.

The eighth house represents the resources you share with others. As the second house defines what you own, the eighth house represents what your partner owns. Here you are confronted with the transformation that results from merging with a partner. The sign on your eighth house describes an attitude that you need to change in order to maintain deep relationships. Planets located in the eighth house often remain hidden until a relationship brings them out.

NINTH HOUSE: In the ninth house one becomes open to the ideas of others. This is where the processes of abstraction and hypothesizing take place. Beliefs and philosophies which form the foundation for rules of conduct by which you wish to guide yourself and others are disseminated here. Agreements are made which become religious codes and laws. There is a desire to share ideas with others in the form of writing and teaching.

In the third house you expanded your communications into your near environment and in the ninth house you expand them into distant or foreign realms. The sign on your ninth house cusp describes your openness to new ideas and philosophies as well as how you prepare yourself to enter society, and the type of higher education you will require.

TENTH HOUSE: The consolidation principle again: Here the consolidation of the beliefs and philosophies from the ninth house leads to the structure of society. There is awareness of the necessity of roles as you develop your place within the whole community. In the tenth house you are confronted with the need to develop your position in the world, a career, profession, or your public reputation and image. How much responsibility you can accept determines these roles and your success in them.

The sign on your tenth house cusp represents qualities that you respect in others and are striving ultimately to incorporate into your own life. It defines your professional or public reputation; the lasting impression that you leave on others. Planets located in the tenth house are strongly highlighted in your profession.

ELEVENTH HOUSE: In the eleventh house there is a banding together with friends and groups of like-minded people for the purpose of creative social reform or political change. This can also manifest as social rebellion. There is a development of group-relatedness where goals are shared in order to contribute to the development of the group. The collectivity of the group's ideas is released through the individual. Structure and adherence to tradition which were developed in the tenth house are transformed into humanitarian expression that will affect all members of the group equally, rather than in the hierarchy found in the tenth house.

The sign on your eleventh house cusp defines your attitudes toward group participation. It also reflects your goals and aspirations, as well as what type of friendship you seek.

TWELFTH HOUSE: To transcend and to dissolve are the two main principles of the twelfth house. There is a need to believe in an existence that transcends what is already known.

This is the last house of the birth chart and it is here that you must face the consequences of all the choices you expressed in the previous houses. You will consolidate your successes into a seed for a new cycle of growth or meet the accumulated results of your failures. Karma, or the collective power of your memories, will be faced in this house of retrospection. Stored karma can be cleared through selfless service to those less fortunate, or may be fled from through drugs, alcohol, and other forms of escapism. Self-limitation needs to be accepted, rather than projected onto others. These self-perceived limitations can be a source of direction if accepted, or frustration if projected.

The sign on the twelfth house cusp describes an attitude that needs adjusting in your personal life, as it has been keeping you from fulfilling your ultimate potential.

Interpreting Astrology

The science of astrology is the casting of an accurate birth chart. It deals with the place, date, and time of birth and reconstructs the celestial environment around that moment. This aspect of astrology is based on verifiable, scientific data, and each astrologer who accurately casts your birth chart will come up with a chart identical to the others.

The interpretation of a birth chart is the art of astrology. It involves combining the hundreds of pieces of information in a chart to interpret their symbolic meaning in your life. Although there are general guidelines which will lead to an overall consistency in chart interpretation, the symbolic nature of a chart lends itself to a great deal of freedom in interpretation.

The accuracy of interpretation of a birth chart is not to be found in the chart itself, it must be verified by the individual living the chart. Does it accurately describe the situation and experiences of the individual? Astrology does not override free will. An astrologer can ascertain what skills, habits, tendencies, resources, and challenges you must integrate into your life. He may even be able to describe people you will encounter, but he cannot say what you will do with all of these variables. That is individual choice (free will).

A good interpretation should be a dialogue between the chart and the individual, via the astrologer. This consists of: 1. projecting what the information in the chart seems to mean, 2. verifying or modifying that postulation by the individual's actual experience, and 3. fitting the actual experience back into the framework of the chart.

If you take the care to modify what you think a symbol should mean in a chart by your actual life experience relevant to that symbol, you will develop a valuable technique for interpretation.

The astrological signs represent needs. They are expressions of energy in specific ways. To have a planet located in a sign means that the specific needs of that sign will color the expression of that planet, forming a natural inclination of the planet's expression. Houses represent areas of life that provide opportunities to meet the needs that the planets in the signs represent.

Let us take for an example a birth chart in which Mars is located in Aries in the ninth house. Mars is the planet which rules passion, drive, and assertion. The sign in which it is found tells how you need to go about getting what you want. Mars, potentially, can be found in any of the twelve signs, but for this example it is in the sign of Aries. Aries rules pioneering, headstrong, impulsive, self-motivated behavior. The ninth house represents the higher mind seeking expression through education, philosophy, travel, and publication. The combination of Mars in Aries in the ninth gives a natural inclination toward being headstrong, impulsive, and assertive in going about higher-mind activities. This person may enjoy debate and challenges expressed through writing articles in publications. It can represent pioneering research and study.

Awareness of the natural inclinations of the combined planets, signs, and houses at birth gives the opportunity to look at these expressions and evaluate how they are being manifested. Astrology does not hold the power to keep you expressing according to your birth chart. This knowledge can either keep you locked into the described mold or offer the stimulus to make you look closer at yourself and want to refine and even change some of these inclinations.

Let's fit this into an analogy with driving an automobile. Let's say this car has some idiosyncrasies, one of which is pulling to the right each time you step on the brake. You are not forced to turn to the right every time you put on the brake, but it is necessary to compensate for your car's inclination in order to prevent that dangerous swerve. It is much the same with astrology. You are not forced to act in the way your signs suggest, but you will have to learn to compensate for your natural inclination.

The prerequisite of compensation is knowledge. Know your vehicle; it's your means of transportation. Each vehicle has its own peculiarities. You will need to probe the depths of your own individuality to discover your uniqueness. Astrology is a model with which you reflect upon yourself; it opens doors to expanded self-awareness. Learning the combinations of your astrological signs, planets, and houses is the opportunity to expand, through compensation, beyond the limitations they could present. Fulfillment is the promise of astrology. By using your birth chart as a map of the multitude of parts of your character, you give yourself the opportunity to integrate their needs and creative potentials into your life.

Suggested Reading

There is a wealth of information written on the subject of astrology, with good-quality publications continually coming out. It would take an interested reader an entire lifetime to read all there is on the subject. The following books are some of our favorites and are representative of various levels of books available.

Arroyo, Stephen. *Astrology, Karma, and Transformation.*
This is one of the real jewels in astrological literature. It is not for beginners as it requires a basic understanding of the language of astrology. Arroyo does a beautiful job of elucidating the meanings of astrology in relationship to the inner dimensions and soul-growth of the individual.

Arroyo, Stephen. *Astrology, Psychology, and the Four Elements.*

Bailey, Alice. *Esoteric Astrology.*

Greene, Liz. *Relating.*
Jungian psychology applied brilliantly to the astrology of relationships. Focuses on how relationship needs and skills can be found within the individual rather than through others.

Ludsted, Betty. *Astrological Insights Into Personality.*
A book for advanced students. Focuses mainly on psychological interpretations of the aspects and the early-childhood responses to these aspects. Excellent book for counselors.

Meyer, Michael. *A Handbook for the Humanistic Astrologer.*

Moore, Marcia and Mark Douglas. *Astrology, the Divine Science.*
One of the better astrology "cookbooks." Includes interpretations for each of the planets in the various signs and houses.

Parker and Parker. *The Complete Astrologer.*
Good, sound astrology in a popular "coffee table" format. This book includes an ephemeris for looking up the planets' positions and is a helpful tool for beginners.

Robertson, Marc. *The Engine of Destiny.*
The definitive work on planets in pairs and phases. This is not a beginner's book; however, it will add depth and insight into the psychological workings of the planetary pairs for all readers.

Robertson, Marc. *Saturn.*
This book goes over the meaning of Saturn in each of its phases with other planets. For anyone interested in the timing and transits of astrology, this is a must.

Rudhyar, Dane. *The Astrology of Personality.*
Many say that this is the book that started it all for modern astrology. Rudhyar has said that all of his astrological thinking is represented in this book. A major, if not the major, astrological publication of the century.

Rudhyar, Dane. *Tryptych.*
All of Rudhyar's work is worth reading, but this philosophical treatise is particularly rewarding. For those interested in the use of astrology as a model of the transformation of consciousness, this book is invaluable.

Wickenburg, Joanne. *A Journey Through the Birth Chart.*
This book teaches the fundamentals of astrology in a very sound and thorough fashion. Excellent for beginners and those not familiar with the language as it starts from ground zero and covers all the essentials in such a way that even advanced students can benefit from it.

Wickenburg, Joanne, and Jinni Meyer. *The Spiral of Life.*

2

Tarot

While I lived in Lahaina, Maui, I met a man who was in the real estate business. When I told him my name, he asked if I was the same one who gave tarot readings above the restaurant and when I said "yes," he said that I had influenced his life a few years ago. He then told me the following story.

Almost two years ago I was preparing to close a very large land sale in Hana, Maui, to a couple from the mainland. They were just at the point of signing the final papers, as we had been going back and forth over the details for several weeks. We were all having coffee in the restaurant below your office when the wife suddenly decided to run upstairs and have a quick tarot reading on this major purchase. When she returned, she announced that the reading clearly said they should not buy this piece of property as nothing good would come from it. The whole project should be dropped immediately. She had asked the same question over and over and the tarot continually gave the same message: "Don't buy the land." They wanted out of the deal immediately. I was furious, as I had already put a lot of time into this, and the deal represented a large sum of

money to me. I tried to persuade
them to change their minds, but
they wouldn't.

As we were talking, he confessed that the land he was trying to
sell them had a "heiau" on it, which is a traditional Hawaiian
holy place. He didn't feel completely comfortable about selling
sacred burial land, but figured he would try to sell it quickly and
never do such a thing again. He didn't mention any of this to the
prospective buyers as he was certain that it wasn't an important
detail anyway. The whole experience was dramatic enough to
make him drop the property and not try to sell any more sacred
land.

...Lucy

The tarot is a deck of seventy-eight cards that have been used
for meditation, divination, entertainment, and fortune-telling.
How they actually work is a topic of much discussion, but that
they do work is generally verified by those who have had readings with the cards or have learned to read the cards themselves.

In all the areas of metaphysics, there is nothing so steeped in
unwarranted mystery as the study of the tarot cards. They are
just a pack of cards with pictures on them. The pictures are fairly
simple representations of life and the many experiences that we
go through in the stages from birth until death. What is so
mysterious or occult about that? The cards are usually straightforward in their presentation of information, yet there are many
decks available ranging from the difficult, which require a manual to understand the symbolism, to the very simple in which the
pictures themselves tell the whole story. In learning to read the
cards, one learns how to connect the various stages of life
experiences with the pictures on each card.

Each of the cards has a picture on it that tells a story through
the use of symbols. Symbols are the language of the right side of
the brain. This is the side of the brain that deals with intuition,
insight, and hunches. It is the other side of the brain, the left
side, that deals with the transmission of rational thought. Tarot
relies heavily on intuition, but there are some left-brain functions that need to be memorized before the process can be

turned over to the right side of the brain. The memorization work involves numerology, basic interpretations of the court cards and major cards, meanings of some of the common symbols, and the layouts of the interpretation patterns.

Of the systems we are presenting in this book, the tarot is unique in that the entire system includes only the cards, the moment in time when you ask the question, and you. To write down the order of a card layout along with your question and present that to a tarot reader who was not present when you asked the question can create some confusion. At that point all the reader has to go on is left-brain memorized meanings of the cards. This interpretation may be of help to you, but you would get a more accurate reading if you and the reader sat and laid out cards together. In this environment the faculty of intuition has more opportunity to surface.

If you have your astrological chart read by several competent astrologers, you will hear much of the same information repeated by each of them. It's the same with palmistry; each of the readings will give approximately the same information. Because the tarot relies so heavily on intuition, this is not so. The meanings of the cards are not fixed and rigid; they can mean different things to different people, depending on the question you have asked, where the cards fall in relation to each other, and the ''energy'' generated by the person asking the question. How all of these variables come together at the time the person is laying out the cards makes up the interpretation itself.

The tarot speaks the language of the subconscious. Each picture triggers the intuitive part of the brain. Much of learning to read the tarot cards is learning to quiet the rational mind that is looking for precise, exact, and consistent meanings for the cards. It is not so much a matter of developing intuition as learning to listen to it. We all have intuition, though it is often a quiet voice. It is like the flute in the orchestra playing next to the cymbals. While both are playing, the flute of intuition fades into the background as the cymbals of rational thought clang loudly away. If you want to hear your intuition, you must quiet the rational mind.

The tarot is most useful for expanding one's perspective. It gives you an opportunity to externalize the situations of your life so that you may objectively look at them represented before you in the layout of the cards. It is a means of broadening your field of consciousness. There are times when it is difficult to see the overview of a situation, and this is exactly when the tarot can prove to be most useful to you. By laying out the cards that symbolically represent the various aspects of your life, you have a chance to see how they are all interrelated.

Misconceptions Concerning The Cards

There are some fears and misconceptions about the cards and their use that need to be addressed. One of the most common misconceptions is that they are fortune-telling cards. The way some people talk about their fear of the cards, it would seem that the cards themselves had some power to dictate the events of one's life. This is not the case any more than the coin used in flipping a coin "decides" which option you will choose. You can let the coin decide your option by *choosing* to let the coin decide, but the choice is still yours. The same is true with the tarot cards. You can prove the cards correct by acting in complete accordance with your reading, or you can choose to do something different. When dealing with tarot cards, it is important to remember that they are most effective when used to expand your perception of what is going on around you. Having the cards represent people, situations, and relationships, you are concerned about can allow you to distance yourself from your emotional involvements long enough to make clear decisions.

How to use the information that comes through a reading is something that takes practice and wisdom. Often you can see trends that you might have otherwise overlooked. Your awareness can be expanded to allow you to see potential trouble spots before they occur and to make decisions out of choice rather than immediacy.

An example is having a reading in which you are concerned about your relationship with your employer. Through the reading you discover that your relationship is less secure than you had expected, and unless some changes are immediately made there is a good chance of losing your job altogether. If you care about maintaining your job, this might cause you to reconsider what you are doing and perhaps develop a new way of approaching your employer. You can walk away from the tarot reading feeling that the information gleaned was helpful in averting a crisis.

Another example is a woman who comes in for a reading concerning the nature of her relationship with her boyfriend. The reading verifies that there is trouble between the two of them and says that if the relationship continues in the same direction, it is leading toward a quick end. If she is in a helpless mood when she leaves, her interpretation of what occurred in the reading might be that there is no hope for her relationship. Because of this, she begins to guard herself emotionally from her boyfriend to keep from being hurt. Because she accepted the reading as the final outcome rather than how to make better choices in the situation, her situation becomes one of self-fulfilling prophecy. She could have chosen to interpret the information that came from the reading as a red flag and started to work harder to improve conditions. That was the option she didn't exercise.

Still another example is the man who says that the tarot is evil because it ruined his marriage. When he was questioned as to how this could have occurred, his response was that he was happily married until his wife went to a tarot reader who said that her husband was a bad influence on her and that she should move away from him immediately. She came home from the reading and did exactly that; she moved away from him. In and of itself, the tarot does not wield that type of power over people's lives. When I heard this story, it occurred to me that more went on in the wife's tarot reading than she had told her husband, and that more difficulties were being experienced in their marriage than he was facing. He was not able to accept either of these theories and continued in his belief that tarot cards are evil. He can choose to make that decision, and try to avoid personal responsibility in the break-up of his marriage, but not seeing his role in the break-up may cause him to repeat the problem.

Another common belief is that you can only use cards that have been given to you. This more than likely stems from a time when knowledge about the cards was handed down by secret societies. To be given a deck of tarot cards was symbolic of having the right to study and use the cards... a right that could not be exercised without this ritual. In these modern times of personal independence, this is no longer the condition. Choosing your own tarot deck can be an exhilarating process. Going to several stores that sell tarot cards and looking at as many decks as you can may be wise before you choose the deck that *feels* right for you.

There is also the belief that your cards should be wrapped in silk and stored in a cedar box. This may be an effective ritual for the care of your cards, but there is nothing to prove that this is what *must* be done.

This is not to say that a ritualistic approach to the cards is wrong. It definitely can be rewarding. The point we are stressing is that there is a difference between superstition and reverence. If there are special ways that you enjoy using and caring for your cards, fine; but if a more casual approach feels right for you, that is all right, too.

De-Mystification Of The Tarot

All of this lore brings up the issue of the right attitudes that are important in the use of all metaphysical systems. The tarot is a tool, and it only has the power and capabilities of the one using the tool. All tools have been misused by some people and handled expertly by others. One can think of terrible ways in which knives have been misused, but that is not a good reason for slicing your bread with a fork. So it is with the tarot. It has been misused by some, but it has also been used with brilliance and sensitivity; its misuse does not make the tarot less valuable as a tool.

The proper attitude for approaching the tarot is a positive frame of mind that is open to gaining information that helps and offers insight. With a positive attitude toward the cards, there needn't be fears surrounding their use. A worthwhile question to consider is: What sort of information do you connect with when using the tarot cards? It resides within you. The information you uncover is always lying just below the level of awareness. Using the tarot helps bring this information to a conscious level.

What To Do Once You Have The Cards

After you have purchased the deck that is appropriate for you, allow yourself some time to get to know your cards. Before you start out with readings it is a good idea to simply get acquainted with your new friends. Look at each one of the cards in the deck and relate the action you see in the cards to everyday experiences. You can easily become confused if you try to absorb too much without practical application. Talking about what you see going on in the cards is the creative part, and the more you familiarize yourself with your cards, the more the symbols will talk to you. Let this process occur. The purpose is to allow the tarot to awaken your sleepy intuition, so don't be shy. Experiment with the cards, and allow yourself to see how they actually reflect your life.

A good way to see the symbols in action is to keep your deck someplace where you spend a lot of time. At different times throughout the day, walk over to the deck and pick a card to symbolize the moment. You will quickly begin to relate various cards with people in your life and familiar situations. This can help bring the cards into a more practical perspective. When you turn over the Strength card with a picture of a lion, you will eventually stop expecting to see real lions in your back yard. The first time you turn over the Devil card you will probably watch closely to see what evil befalls you, and perhaps become suspicious as the day comes and goes with no horrible event to cope with. The Devil card is more subtle than that, usually symbolizing negative thinking that is difficult to shake. With time and experience, the symbols will readily be translated into common-life meanings.

Tarot Journal

Part of the getting-acquainted process involves translating the symbols into representations of situations and people in your own life. A good way of accelerating this process is to keep a journal of your new-found awareness. Picking a card to represent the moment or the day and then writing about what it actually symbolizes is a good way to stimulate your intuition. Whole readings can also be recorded, dated, and then written about. As the months go by you will begin to see combinations of cards repeated which refer to very specific situations. Ultimately, this journal will teach you more about your unconscious and intuition than any other book.

Retrospective Fortune-Telling

Although the cards have the reputation of being used for pre-
dicting the future, we have found that their greatest use is in
understanding the past. For the sincere searcher, the tarot can
help uncover personal motivations and hidden lessons from
past experiences. It is often through a better understanding of
the past that we are able to grow and accept teachings that are
not so apparent in the present. The tarot always shows why we
are being confronted by a problem and what adjustments we
need to make in order to move beyond it. If you are willing to
explore the hidden aspects of your own psyche, the tarot is truly
a remarkable way.

When To Use The Cards

*When I first began using the tarot, I followed all of the pre-
scribed methods for keeping the cards pure, and then some.
Since I wanted to give REALLY good readings, I wanted to
approach them with the right attitude. I built a little driftwood
altar in my bedroom and sat in front of it when I used the cards. I
never used the cards in the presence of other people. In fact, no
one else was allowed to see or touch my deck. I purified myself
with a shower before I used them. I would never use them if I
had indulged in any stimulants, including coffee, tobacco or
alcohol. The net result was that I got to use them very little! After
realizing the limitations of my self-imposed rituals, I decided to
"lighten up" and found that anytime is a good time for reading
the cards.*

...David

How The Tarot Works

Learning to read the cards is both a creative and a technical
process. Insights are born through the interaction of the reader
with the symbols represented in the cards. When the psyche
allows the symbols to be uncritically received, the function of

intuition happens spontaneously. This intuitive recombining of the symbols leads automatically to insights and expanded per- spectives in relation to the situation being explored by the cards.

There is a right time and a right place for study of the tarot and the subsystems that make up the whole, but it is not while you are giving a reading. Study before and after your readings, but not during. Trying to remember what a card means blocks the spontaneity that a good reading requires. Set aside your studies while you are reading the cards and allow the symbols to act freshly on your intuition. This is not as easy as it sounds. We are so conditioned by our education system to want to know the right answer and not make mistakes, that it becomes a chal- lenge to accept the belief that the right answer is always just below the level of conscious thought.

Confidence is hard to come by when you first begin with the tarot. The methods used to build this confidence have to do with lots of practice and learning to integrate the cards into your everyday life. Retrospective study of your tarot journal will add more depth as to how the tarot actually works in your own life.

Structure Of The Tarot

The tarot is made up of seventy-eight cards. Of these, twenty- two are called major cards and the other fifty-six are the minor cards. Within the minor cards there are sixteen court cards, four to each suit. There are many good tarot decks available, but we are using the Waite deck of cards as a point of reference in this chapter.

78 Cards

22 major cards	56 minor cards
Fool's Journey	*4 suits of 14 cards*

SUBSYSTEMS WITHIN THE TAROT: By familiarizing your- self with the subsystems represented within the tarot, you can see how the various cards received their meanings. At first, the meanings appear random and chaotic, but with a basic exposure to these systems you will be able to see how the various authors and artists came up with the meanings and images that appear on the cards.

Numerology And The Tarot

Numerology is one of the core components of the tarot. Numbers are a repetitive cycle, and each one leads to the next as a natural step in the process. At this point it will be most helpful if you memorize one or two keywords for each of the numbers, as this information will help you greatly with your interpretations. A chapter of this book has been devoted to the study of numbers, but the following keywords will give you a vocabulary with which to begin.

Each of the minor cards has a number from ace, or 1, to 10 written on it. Each of these numbers represents a stage of development the theme of the suit represents. By familiarizing yourself with the attributes of each of the numbers, you will be able to formulate beginning interpretations for each of the cards without having to look up their meanings. The keywords point out where to look.

ACE: Beginning, initiation, potential of the suit. Hand out of the sky, not anchored in the real world. Something new exists. It is not yet manifest, simply potential.

2: Reflection, opposition, duality, realization of choice. Comparing one option to another. Balance.

3: Expansion, growth, preparation for the future. Enthusiasm. There is now more perspective to make a decision than with a #2.

4: Structure, foundation, form, realization, work. Solid and stable. Reward through effort.

5: Uncertainty, strife, flux, adjustment and adaptation. Whatever was established in a #4 is now being challenged. Change is required.

6: Harmony, balance, peace, appreciation and indulgence. Personal values are formed and defended.

7: Change, intuition, aloofness, rebellion. Expanded awareness. Opportunity to stand back and witness your experience.

8: Activity, organization, enterprise, power, and control. Solidity; it's your test in a chance for recognition.

9: Dreamy, compassionate. Martyrdom. Wisdom and understanding. Prepare for transition.

10: Completion, or the end of the cycle. Regeneration. You have gone as far as you can; now you must make a transformation.

When looking at a minor card for meanings, it is helpful to use these keywords for the numbers along with your understanding of the general meanings of the suits. The combination will help you know which areas of life require your attention. Then look to the symbols within the card to stimulate the intuition for added information on what the card means to your particular inquiry.

EXAMPLE: You are interpreting the Four of Wands. Even without looking at the picture you can tell quite a bit about the meaning of the card by simply combining the keyword for the #4, which is realization, and the keyword for the suit of wands, which is aspiration. The Four of Wands denotes realization of aspirations.

Images As Symbols

The artwork within the tarot is symbolic. The images represented in the cards are not random choices, but have particular meanings. As you continue your study with the tarot, you will continually unearth new symbols to incorporate in your interpretations. To begin, it is helpful to memorize the meanings of the most general types of symbols that appear in many of the cards. Later you will develop your eye for detail and want to study the meanings of specific symbols that are found only in a few of the cards. Following is a list of the more common symbols and their meanings:

ANGELS: Higher self. Angels represent the source of inspiration and guidance. Inspiration is available if the person can listen to his or her higher mind.

ANIMALS: Lower self. Biological urges that need to be tempered by the higher self. Anger, passion, vindictiveness, and greed.

BUILDINGS: Security. What has been achieved and built. Typically, this is material security rather than emotional or spiritual. Notice where any people are in relation to the buildings. Are they approaching or moving away from their established security?

CLOUDS: Emotions. The more jagged the clouds, the more irritable the emotions. Big, full, fluffy clouds represent contentment and joy.

HILLS: Minor challenges. These represent tasks that are not too difficult to overcome.

MOUNTAINS: Challenges. Notice where they are located in the card; way off in the distance, or close at hand. This is the way of knowing how far away or close your challenges lie. Also notice the color of the mountain as this further qualifies the nature of the task.

RISING SUN: Improving condition. Renewal.

RIVERS: Movement of consciousness. Rapidly moving rivers suggest surrendering to the flow that is moving around you. Still water represents the stagnation of consciousness.

ROCKS: Annoyances, disturbances, minor challenges that need to be kicked out of the way or gone around.

SETTING SUN: End of a situation.

WATER: Movement of consciousness. The condition of the water is symbolic of your emotional state. See Rivers.

Colors As Symbols

Interpretation clues can also be gained from noticing the colors within the cards themselves and noticing if a spread of cards has a predominance of a particular color. Again, remember the properties and apply them uniquely to each situation rather than memorizing their meanings in a static form. Following is a list of the seven main colors and their attributes. We have also included the correspondences of colors to chakras. The chakras are described in the chapter on Applied Metaphysics, to which you may refer.

RED: Chakra: root or base of the spine. Effect on the body: gives physical strength and stamina. Aids in circulation of the blood. Stimulates the senses and arouses sensuality. Heats the body, effective in offsetting chills. Red "longjohns" are a use of this principle. Effect on the metaphysical body: promotes impulsive behavior. Causes one to become more aggressive or assertive. Gives confidence and a sense of power. Stimulates anger.

EXAMPLE: The red outer robe on the Magician shows the ability to use the power of the will when needed, and yet the robe is easily taken off, showing how the Magician can relax personal will when it is not required.

ORANGE: Chakra: sacral or sexual. Effect on the body: stimulates the spleen, liver and pancreas. Increases vitality. Increases gland activity. Stimulates the thyroid and aids the lungs. Increases elimination of all bodily discharges. Aids in digestion and assimilation of food. Effect on the metaphysical body: helps break past conditioning. Many sannyasins of eastern religions wear this color exclusively to aid in breaking their ties with the past. Gives courage.

EXAMPLE: The orange lion in the strength card shows the vitality and sexual magnetism that is available when one tames the instincts with the higher mind.

YELLOW: Chakra: solar plexus. Effect on the body: increases mental activity. Stimulates the intellect and the nervous system. Strengthens logic and reasoning power. Aggravates nervousness. Effect on metaphysical body: improves disposition. Aids in discernment and discriminative use of the will.

EXAMPLE: The yellow star in the Star card shows the elevation of the spirit and the clarity of mind that is available at this stage of consciousness.

GREEN: Chakra: heart. Effect on the body: brings about balance to restore rest and relaxation. Calms the sympathetic nervous system. Clears head colds and calms hay fever. Effect on the metaphysical body: heals emotional tangles and soothes nerves. Stimulates love and generosity. Opens the heart to universal acceptance. Promotes stability and harmony.

EXAMPLE: The green cloak on the shoulders of the person in the Justice card shows the discernment of harmony and balance that this card refers to. Green promotes a sense of generosity.

BLUE: Chakra: throat. Effect on the body: breaks fevers, lowers pulse and promotes sleep. Soothes the mind. Lowers blood pressure. Astringent and cooling effect. Effect on the metaphysical body: promotes creativity, devotion, and idealism. Provides inspiration for the spirit. Brings peace and quiet. Conversely, when a person is blocked from inspiration, the "blues" are experienced.

EXAMPLE: The blue robes of the High Priestess refer to the devotion and faith that she encourages.

INDIGO: Chakra: pituitary. Effect on the body: minimal effect on the physical body, works mostly on the metaphysical plane. Effect on the metaphysical body: stimulates intuition, telepathy and the ability to mind travel. Promotes self-mastery. Removes fears. Gives a desire for service to mankind.

VIOLET: Chakra: pineal, crown. Effect on the body: tranquilizing. Draws one farthest away from physical-body awareness. Effect on the metaphysical body: promotes spiritual mastery. Purifies the will. Transforms personal ego into godliness. Promotes humanitarian goals. Used for spiritual protection.

EXAMPLE: The dancing figure in the World card is clothed only in a violet scarf showing the spiritual mastery and attainment that this card refers to.

The Four Suits

In understanding the four suits, it is helpful to realize that each suit represents one function of the personality. Before looking at the cards to discover what they relate to, look to yourself. Identify the function of the suit with the corresponding function of your own personality.

The division of the human personality into four categories is common practice. Carl Jung used this division in his famous model of the cornerstones of the personality. In his model, he stated that the personality functions through four vehicles: intuition, sensation, thinking, and feeling.

In astrology, this fourfold division is also found in the elements. These groups correspond in the following way:

Tarot	Astrological	Psychological
SUIT	ELEMENT	FUNCTION
Wands	Fire	Intuiting
Pentacles	Earth	Sensing
Swords	Air	Thinking
Cups	Water	Feeling

THE SUIT OF WANDS:

The leaders. Inspirational and enthusiastic.
The Fire signs: Aries, Leo, Sagittarius.
Clubs in a regular deck of playing cards.

Positive personality characteristics: warm, friendly, outgoing, original, proud, energetic, spontaneous, magnetic, inspiring, extroverted. Enjoys a challenge.

Negative personality characteristics: aggressive, pushy, arrogant, impulsive, headstrong, selfish, dogmatic, impatient, temperamental.

KEYWORDS FOR THE SUIT: personality, self-image, self-identity. Aspirations, careers, enterprise, and ambition. Inspiration, will power, sense of direction, and purpose. Pride, friendship, and expansion.

PROFESSIONS: artist, teacher, leaders within a field. Athletic and competitive. Careers that offer a challenge and personal freedom. Entertainers.

NATURE OF THE SUIT: making plans about the future.

THE SUIT OF SWORDS:

The thinkers. Intellectuals. Head over heart.
The Air signs: Gemini, Libra, Aquarius.
Spades in a regular deck of playing cards.

Positive personality characteristics: perceptive, versatile, flexible, sociable, communicative, mentally alert, extroverted. Likes lively exchange of ideas.

Negative personality characteristics: superficial, changeable, restless, nervous, scattered, indecisive, argumentative, cold.

KEYWORDS FOR THE SUIT: communication, thoughts and ideas. Objectivity, detachment, all workings of the mind. Opinions and strife. Separation, fear and struggle. Although the negativity in the sword cards is not a fair reflection of the Air signs, the tarot shows that negativity is often a product of the mind.

PROFESSIONS: lawyer, writer, speaker, teacher. All fields that involve communication or movement of ideas.

NATURE OF THE SUIT: to disseminate ideas. Networking.

THE SUIT OF CUPS:

The nurturers, emotionally expressive.
The Water signs: Cancer, Scorpio, Pisces.
Hearts in a regular deck of playing cards.

Positive personality characteristics: artistic, imaginative, intuitive, sensitive, compassionate, maternal, receptive, domestic. Live more on feelings than on logic. Warm and loving.

Negative personality characteristics: moody, lazy, dependent, possessive, unrealistic, unreliable, secretive, hypersensitive, violent, daydreamers. Fearful and overly cautious.

KEYWORDS FOR THE SUIT: feelings, emotions, love and happiness. Spiritual well-being. Compulsive, indulgent. Habit patterns. Intuitive and psychic. Procreation, home, friendship , and family.

PROFESSIONS: artists, doctors, priests, counselors, and careers in the helping professions. Homemaking.

NATURE OF THE SUIT: to experience the emotions.

THE SUIT OF PENTACLES:

The doers. Realistic and practical. Result-seekers.
The Earth signs: Taurus, Virgo, Capricorn.
Diamonds in a regular deck of playing cards.

Positive personality characteristics: responsible, trusting, reliable, patient, honest, organized, serious, quiet, dependable, conventional. Introverted. Sensual. Task-oriented, successful.

Negative personality characteristics: materialistic, dull, limited, stubborn, miserly, worrisome, rigid, pessimistic, greedy, fearful, opportunistic.

KEYWORDS FOR THE SUIT: business, finance, money. Material gain or loss. Financial transactions. Inheritance. Enjoyment of the senses. Values. All that is tangible.

PROFESSIONS: business, commerce, and farming. Entrepreneur-executive positions. Maintenance, repair and construction. Restaurateur.

It can be seen that four suits fall into two major groupings. The Wand and Sword suits are both masculine in nature, dealing with abstract energy. They are primarily active and work with spirit and ideas. The Pentacle and Cup suits are feminine in nature, dealing with emotional energy and form. These two suits are interested in the product and the content of experience.

Some Basic Interpretations Of The Minor Cards

WANDS:

Ace: New beginnings, plans for the future, a good idea.

2: Waiting; contemplation of the future.

3: A valuable perspective concerning the future.

4: Manifestation of a dream; beauty and happiness.

5: Confusion, going in too many different directions.

6: Harmony, creative confidence. Pride in your work.

7: Stiff competition, new responsibilities. A test.

8: Passage of time is required for fruition. New growth.

9: Reticence. Wisdom through awareness of past mistakes.

10: Overburdened, no time for individual expression.

PENTACLES:

Ace: Business opportunity, job offer, unexpected money.

2: Situation is not "either/or" at this time, it is both.

3: Progress. Growth and expansion.

4: Tenaciously holding on to what you have.

5: Spiritual or financial uncertainty. Poor health.

6: Balance finances: pay bills, collect debts.

7: Task is not complete; important detail overlooked.

8: Continued efforts bring success. Need for organization.

9: Wisdom, material success. Comfort.

10: Strong family ties. Completion of material task.

SWORDS:

Ace: New idea or new way of thinking. A letter.

2: Both choices are the same; make no decision.

3: Separation, delay, broken heart.

4: Meditate; rest is needed.

5: Verbal battle, loss of friends. Mental tension.

6: Movement toward peace. Journey by water.

7: Distraction; analyze motivations.

8: Blinded by your own thoughts. Mentally trapped.

9: Guilt over past situation. Nightmare.

10: The worst is over. Let go of the situation completely.

CUPS:

Ace: Birth, new love. New hope. Optimism.

2: Affirmation of good relationship. Balance. Agreement.

3: Celebration of abundance. Joyful sharing.

4: Daydreaming, an offer may go by unnoticed.

5: Disappointment. Let go of past, focus on what remains.

6: Innocence. Childlike sharing. Reincarnational tie.

7: Ungrounded fantasy or creative visualization. Need to assign priority to your options.

8: Solitude is needed to realign with emotional cycles.

9: You will get what you want; be careful of your wishes.

10: Emotional fulfillment. Completion. Family ties.

Court Cards

Court cards are neither major cards nor minor cards; they stand in a class by themselves. They most often represent actual people in your life, but they can also represent different attributes of your self. Frequent use of your cards will ultimately be the way you will discover what they actually mean to you.

Many of the lessons we are learning in life are brought to us through other people. Sigmund Freud first labeled this process "projection." It is the process of projecting what you are working on, consciously or subconsciously, onto the other people in your life. The court cards represent these projections.

There are four court cards in each suit, two female and two male. The page and queen are the females, and the knight and king are the males. The page generally represents one who is interested in developing the attributes of the suit but is at a naive and immature state of development. The knight, who is always shown on a horse, represents one who is actively pursuing those qualities. The king and the queen represent the mature development of the qualities of the suit.

When the court cards do not represent actual people in your life, they can signify a level of accomplishment relative to your question.

KING: Mastery and control. Represents a person, usually a man, who is respected in his field of expression and has attained a certain position of authority. Can be assertive and demanding.

QUEEN: Represents an older, accomplished person, usually a woman. Maturity and competence are present.

KNIGHT: An aggressive urge to discover one's abilities using whatever suit the card symbolizes. Acting out of haste. Strong determination is present. The armor protects vulnerability.

PAGE: Messengers. Youthful person or enterprise. Young boy or girl or child. New involvement. Immature plan.

Major Cards

The cards of the major arcana represent the inner psychological processes or spiritual lessons in life. One of the most beneficial ways to understand the major cards is to consider them as a story. In this way, each card assumes significance as part of the whole.

It can be enlightening to look at the story of the Fool's Journey through the major arcana as a model of the human relationship to the surrounding universe. It is both a tool for developing a greater understanding of the uses of tarot and an excellent model for organizing your personal awareness. For ease in reading the story, it is told in the masculine; but of course it applies to the feminine as well.

Fool's Journey

Within the major arcana of the tarot is one of the oldest stories of the human experience. Because the tarot is presented in a symbolic form, it can at first appear a complex task to decode the total story; but it is actually a simple tale which describes the continuous cyclic process of growth experienced by all of us.

As the story begins, the soul is in spirit form: pure, unmanifested energy. Here, as THE FOOL, our wayfarer begins the journey of life with knapsack on his shoulder, eyes gazing at the heavens, one foot on the ground and the other foot in the air. He is at the top of a precipice, and as his raised foot comes down, he will naively tumble into a new world of experience. Within his knapsack he carries all the tools necessary for his journey.

With his first step, he experiences the world of THE MAGICIAN. Here the Fool learns the seemingly magical process of the spirit world becoming manifest. He is given access to the tools he is carrying, and a will to create. The Magician's role is to teach our Fool how to focus the creative energy flowing through him. The Fool must learn how to align his will with the universal will, as that is the source of his creative power.

To balance this outpouring of energy, THE HIGH PRIESTESS becomes his next teacher. From her he must learn faith and trust in order to be penetrated with and guided by spirit. Receptivity is the key, and acceptance is the path.

Continuing on this path, his next step is into the world of the senses. The physical plane is represented here by THE EMPRESS. Our Fool now finds himself in the world of fertility and abundance, which is enjoyable and tempts our traveler to tarry too long in experiences of sensuality.

Strength and direction are required to keep the Fool moving, but his passions have now been awakened, so his next lesson must teach him to control these inflamed passions. THE EMPEROR shows him how to gain power by controlling not only his emotions, but all aspects of his life. The gift of the Emperor is the two-edged sword of power. The temptation to use this instrument for only his own good must be overcome before the Fool can continue on his path to discover the world.

Having experienced both sides of passion (the passion for life through the Empress and the passion for power through the Emperor) the Fool is thrown back to his roots, and is engulfed by a memory of all that has been previously experienced. This prepares him for his encounter with THE HIEROPHANT, where he is offered the wisdom of those who have passed before him. Sanctity in the traditions and conventions of religion is the enticement of this stop.

Now our youthful traveler has experienced two sides of his nature. The Empress and the Emperor taught him of the pleasures of the material world and the Hierophant exposed him to the world of spiritual comforts. Integration is the principle he must learn from THE LOVERS. Through the awareness of duality and the attraction of opposites, he sees that he is made up of light and dark forces, the "yin" and the "yang," and that both are necessary components of wholeness.

Gaining mastery over these light and dark forces is what must be accomplished next. The lesson of THE CHARIOT is how to handle the ups and downs of life with equal dexterity. This course is guided by using the invisible reins of his will to balance the constant riddle of opposites perceived by his senses.

Becoming more aware of the subtle laws of nature gives our Fool inner STRENGTH. This card shows a woman calmly closing the jaws of a lion. Love, compassion and a sense of control originating in her higher consciousness are all she needs to tame this beast, showing the strength hidden in softness. The realization that spirit can conquer matter marks the beginning of spiritual awareness.

From this point onward, the action will be less spontaneous and more deliberate. With the new awakening of the guiding power of consciousness, the Fool is ready for the teachings of the HERMIT. The Hermit instructs the traveler that the esoteric knowledge he is now learning is not meant to be hidden from the masses, but to gain the esoteric knowledge, one has to search in areas where the masses are not typically found. The inner light he is gaining from his experiences isolates him from the common path. His first feelings of aloneness are erased by the peace of all-oneness which inner tranquility brings.

Next comes the lesson of the WHEEL OF FORTUNE and the dramatic changes of fate. Here the Fool learns that no matter how centered he stays, life continues to change. When he stays centered, all the changes are like spokes on a wheel: separate but united at the hub. He begins to learn of the retribution of karma: what he sows he will also reap. He sees that each step is laying the foundation for the next step. This causes him to consider the consequences of his actions more thoroughly.

The Fool is made aware that there is a certain JUSTICE in the way the wheel of life moves for each person. He is able to see definite themes in what once appeared to be random changes. Now he sees that he is bound by inner laws.

At this point, his awareness of spiritual laws serves more as a form of bondage than as a basis for freedom; his consciousness has been awakened. At the stage of THE HANGED MAN, he is very aware of what he can and can't do if he is to remain centered and in balance with his karma. He knows what interferes with his enlightenment and is quite willing to make sacrifices to maintain his spiritual identity. The challenge is one of expressing his individuality in the face of possible ostracism, without falling into the role of a martyr. The Hanged Man shows the Fool the fine line between real and imagined limitations of spiritual identity.

Now our maturing traveler has found his individual path to enlightenment. At this point, others seem like a deterrent to spiritual progress. This attitude must undergo a certain DEATH in order for him to progress on his journey. He is shown that he must let go of all attitudes that restrict his interaction with others. The lesson is that in order to be reborn and continue to evolve, he must be willing to let his previous concepts of self and life die. Evolution and transformation are the means, and confrontation with the self is the method.

Undergoing the death of previous consciousness has brought the Fool a new awareness. Now he must balance and integrate his physical and spiritual lives. He is shown that he must have a firm footing on the material plane before he can wade into the waters of consciousness. It is time to plan carefully and realign reality with ideals. This is the teaching of TEMPERANCE. He cannot move ahead until his objectives become more clear and he has fully integrated all that he has learned.

This brings on his confrontation with THE DEVIL. "Use it or lose it" is the name of the game here. It is not enough to know of spiritual laws; if they are not integrated and activated, he will succumb to the temptations put before him by the Devil. It is easy for the mind to become cluttered and only see that which it fears losing. These fears are played upon by the Devil, and unless the Fool is strong, his development will be held in check by negative thinking patterns. If he can deny the power of negativity and refuse to be ruled by his own weaknesses, he will move on.

Next, THE TOWER will sweep away everything in the Fool's life that is not needed for the journey ahead. Unexpected disruptions and threats to basic security help the Fool distinguish between things of lasting value and those that are only temporarily satisfying. The energy of the Tower is like a bolt of spiritual awakening that purges our Fool of everything in his life that is not built on a solid foundation of value. This cleansing is so intense that it is hard for him to immediately adjust, but gradually the experience flows into an awakening.

Stripped of all the illusionary aspects of life, the Fool is able to see THE STAR of his own enlightenment. Now that his senses are uncluttered with attachments to physical pleasures, he is able to become a clear channel to receive inspiration from his higher consciousness. He learns that there can be bondage not only to things, but to thoughts as well. To receive true inspiration, he has to learn to quiet his mind.

A new danger befalls the Fool. By quieting his mind, he was able to get in touch with forces beyond himself. This brought the risk of attachment to these new psychic abilities. What he must learn now is to relax and be like THE MOON: reflecting the light that he receives. By quieting his mind, he sees that his intuition can go far beyond the boundaries of logical thinking. Thus he learns a new facet of himself: his task on earth is to make himself a clearer and purer reflection of the wisdom that is already in the world. This is the last phase of self-doubt.

Now THE SUN comes shining through with radiance. Our Fool is becoming innocent and joyous. Like a child, he is ready to experience the fullness of life. He starts as a child, and he must leave as a child. It has been a long road back to the state of innocence for our traveler, but he is not bitter, exhausted or too tired to continue. Quite the opposite is true. He is now riding on the wave of solar energy and is swept along in a direction that he is glad to follow.

By becoming what is possible for all to become, our transformed traveler now can hear the trumpet of JUDGMENT. He realizes that the trumpet was sounding all the time, but by his own actions he was never able to hear it until now. He is shown that the Day of Judgment is ever-present and that he, as well as all beings, is a product of his own actions. This awareness has opened up the locked doors of his mind and he is now able to receive direct guidance from his higher self.

The next step is the last before the cycle repeats itself. The final step is THE WORLD. The World itself is the same but our traveler has grown and sees it all with new eyes. He now has consciousness to take with him, and he will dance through the universe with newly gained awareness. Our traveler is ready to emerge into the world of spirit, again as the Fool, ready to start another cycle of incarnation.

Basic Interpretations Of The Major Arcana

0 THE FOOL: New beginnings. You have a decision to make; an opportunity to try something completely new. A new direction is open to you. Move on faith.

1 THE MAGICIAN: Access to tremendous power. Strong self-motivation is present. Express your individuality with courage. All the tools you need are before you to be used in a balanced way.

2 THE HIGH PRIESTESS: Hidden issues; a test of patience. The situation is not what it appears. Trust your intuition and sense of right timing for guidance. Unseen assistance.

3 THE EMPRESS: Fruitful experience. Sensual pleasure. Abundance. A fertile situation promises growth. Indulgence. Potential birth.

4 THE EMPEROR: Authoritarian attitude. A person who can be dogmatic, unyielding and stubborn. Exert your will. Time to put form and structure into your plans.

5 THE HIEROPHANT: Traditional search for spiritual values and meaning.

6 THE LOVERS: Magnetic attraction and human love are present. Friendship and courtship. You will attract what you desire, be it business or romance.

7 THE CHARIOT: Travel. Moving forward as you handle the ups and downs of life through the balanced use of your will. Continue on your path. Mastery of opposites.

8 STRENGTH: Will power. You will develop strength through this situation. Control your desires. Lower nature is brought into harmony with higher self.

9 THE HERMIT: Solitude. Separation from others is required to restore inner balance. Listen to the quiet voice within. Guidance is available.

10 THE WHEEL OF FORTUNE: All things must pass; the situation is not stable. Expect a change. Life is in perpetual change; prepare to adapt.

11 JUSTICE: Karmic retribution. A time for inner adjustment and the use of good judgment. Restore balance. An unfinished lesson from the past reappears.

12 THE HANGED MAN: Enlightenment through limitation. Trust your inner voice. Sacrifice pleasures now for later spiritual rewards. Remain true to inner goals even in the face of questioning by those around you. Though the Hanged Man is upside down, he is comfortable. He is in a yoga posture and there is a halo around his head.

13 DEATH: Transformation and regeneration. A time when something of importance is passing away. Let go of the past. The situation is over. Prepare for rebirth.

14 TEMPERANCE: Moderation, compromise. Expand yourself through blending of high ideals with reality. You must be patient and wait. Integration.

15 DEVIL: Deep-seated passions, indulgences, and ignorance. A challenge to your weaknesses. If you are feeling chained to a person or a situation it is because you CHOOSE to be. Notice that the chains are loosely placed around their necks; they can be removed easily. Let go of attachments.

16 THE TOWER: Drastic, sudden change in situation. A shake-up. All that is of no value will fall away. Expect a break-up of crystallized patterns.

17 THE STAR: Honesty, clarity. Insight, hope, and truth are present. Trust your intuition. Reputation is on the upswing. What has been promised will come to pass.

18 THE MOON: Mental unrest. The emergence of repressed tendencies from the unconscious. Psychic powers emerge as you learn to separate the real from the imagined. Move ahead with caution. Hidden forces are at work.

19 THE SUN: Vitality, zest, enthusiasm. Strong direction toward a conscious purpose brings good fortune. Be joyous. Life is moving in a direction that you want. Enjoy the ride!

20 JUDGMENT: Spiritual awakening. Benefit for all concerned. Revelation of truth. There is an urge to uplift the total personality. The decision has been made.

21 THE WORLD: Harmonious molding of earthly powers and spiritual values. You have reached the end of this particular cycle. Celebration of right use of power.

Reversed Cards

The question often arises as to how one interprets reversed or upside-down cards in a reading. Some sources suggest reversing the meaning of the card. If it is a positive card originally, it becomes negative when reversed. Another approach is to treat each card as both positive and negative so that each card has a 360-degree range of how it can be experienced. When we come to a reversed card in our readings, we turn them upright to provide a better view. Since it takes extra effort to view the card correctly, we incorporate that in the interpretation. The reversed card symbolizes a situation or attitude that might not be perceived correctly by the person. Also, since extra effort was required to see the card correctly, we go to extra effort in ferreting out its meaning.

Preparing To Read The Cards

Beginners might first get a flash of insight into what a card means in their lives, and then the conscious mind interrupts... "No, it just couldn't be that." Next, they start looking for answers with the conscious mind. Well, it not only could BE "that," it often IS "that." Your first impression is what the cards are designed to stimulate, and the art of learning to read your tarot cards is directly related to the art of listening to your intuition. With more and more practice you begin to trust this information.

When asking a question of the tarot, first meditate on the question so you are fully aware of what you are asking. Once you are clear on this, concentrate on it as you shuffle the cards. When you feel the cards are shuffled, cut them into three piles: toward you if the question is personal, and away from you if you are seeking information on another person or on a situation that is external to you. As you pick up your cards, ask yourself for understanding and insight. This prayer is amazingly effective and should not be overlooked.

If you are reading for another person there is an additional focus in your pre-reading meditation that can be very helpful. As you are asking your higher self for understanding, acknowledge that you have your own personal problems, but would like to temporarily place them aside so that you may be a clear channel for the other person. This helps in alleviating the "superman" complex that many readers fall into by feeling that they must be perfect in order to help others. Acknowledging your personal problems lowers the risk of reading your own problems into the other person's cards.

Methods Of Divination Using The Tarot

With proper knowledge the tarot can give:

1. Insight into daily problems
2. Spiritual guidance
3. Meditational awareness

There are various methods of laying out the cards. These are called "spreads." The different types of spreads are useful for different types of questions. Following are the most popular spreads and the types of questions they address.

The Yes/No Spread

This spread only deals with questions that can be answered with a "yes" or "no." It is useful as an indicator of whether an event is likely to happen or not. Sample questions: "Will John be visiting me as promised?" or, "Will Grace accept the offer?"

This is a three-card reading. The person asking the question shuffles the cards while thinking of the question and then cuts the cards into two piles. The portion of the deck that you moved to the left should be turned upright. The portion of the deck on the right is still face down. Take the top card off the right-hand pile and turn it face up, placing it between the two piles. Now you have two cards showing, and the top card of the right-side pile still face down. The final step is to turn the top card of the right-side pile face up so there are three cards showing.

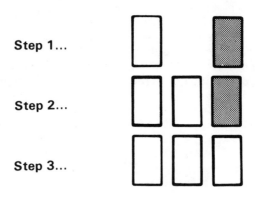

Step 1...

Step 2...

Step 3...

Some source books say to interpret the reading by seeing if the majority of the cards are reversed or upright. We have found this too logical for the tarot which is an interpretive rather than logical art.

While interpreting, it is important to get a *feel* for the cards. Are they generally positive, suggesting a "yes," or are they generally negative, suggesting a "no?" Or is it both positive and negative, making it hard to decide, suggesting the outcome is yet undecided?

With some practice you not only can answer the basic yes or no, but you should also be able to qualify the answer with a few *hows*. This can be done by interpreting the story of each of the cards individually.

EXAMPLE: Question: "Will I complete the project I've started?"

Cards: 3 of Swords, Judgment, Ace of Cups.

Interpretation: Two of the cards seem positive; Judgment and the Ace of Cups. The 3 of Swords seems negative. The overall balance seems to imply that it is still undecided but that the potential is good. Further interpretation of the individual cards would say that there are some frustrations due to delays (3 of Swords). However, the person should become re-inspired (Judgment), and will probably develop some new feelings about the project (Ace of Cups).

Expanded Three-Card Reading: Follow all of the above steps. To add to your interpretation, notice that the card on the extreme left is the PAST, the middle card is the PRESENT, and the card on the far right is the FUTURE of the situation you asked about.

The Horoscope Spread

This is an excellent exploratory spread for gathering information. It is designed to reflect the energy surrounding an individual. The twelve houses of astrology are used for the positions of the cards. While interpreting, you combine the meaning of the card with reference to the astrological house in which it is found. One card in the center is a tie-in card to all the others and represents a central theme.

Procedures:

1. Shuffle the cards.

2. Cut the cards 3 times and then reincorporate them into one deck.

3. Take the first card off the pile and place it in the center. This is the significator or central theme card.

4. Place one card in each of the twelve positions, beginning with the first house and continuing in a counter-clockwise direction until each of the 12 positions has a card.

5. Interpret each card with regard to its placement.

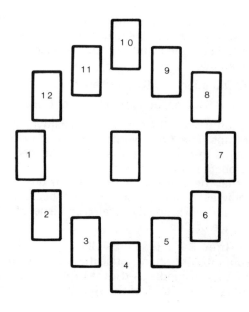

SIGNIFICATOR: This card represents the person or situation that the rest of the cards refer to.

CARD 1: Projection of self to others.

CARD 2: Your security, self-worth, resources, values, and money.

CARD 3: What's on your mind. Siblings. How you communicate.

CARD 4: Roots, foundation, family, and home. Self-image.

CARD 5: Creative pursuits, risks, children, fun, and romance.

CARD 6: Health. Job. Day-to-day routines.

CARD 7: Marriage, partnerships.

CARD 8: Shared resources. Taxes. Psychological merging with partner.

CARD 9: Need to expand. Higher education. Religious and philosophical pursuits.

CARD 10: Your image in the public eye. Reputation, career, and profession.

CARD 11: Aspirations for the future. Friends. Group involvement.

CARD 12: Impact of accumulated past on present. Karma.

Interpretation Clues:

Looking at the layout as a whole can give you some valuable insights. Is there a dominance of one suit? That can show a dominant theme affecting the person at this time. Is there a lack of a particular suit? This can show an area of life that is being neglected or overlooked by the person. Is there a disproportionate number of major cards? If there is more than you would expect from random generation it suggests an inner psychological focus. If there are more minor cards than you would expect, then it is the mundane affairs of life that concern the person at this time.

As in all readings, remember that the minor cards describe events and people encountered. These represent situations over which you have control. The major cards tell of the inner psychological meanings and significance of events. These are generally situations over which you do not have control.

Ask questions as they come into your mind; this is a good way to pick up impressions. Don't stumble over cards. If they don't say anything to you, just move past that card and work with a card that is talking to you. Don't persist to get answers; there are situations that you will not be able to sort out. Practice often. Learn to communicate your impressions.

Keep In Mind:

    1. The meaning of the card
    2. The position in the spread
    3. How it relates to the question

The Celtic Cross Spread

The procedure is the same as other spreads. Focus on the question as you shuffle the cards. Cut them into three piles. Cut with your right hand, and then pick them back up with the left to integrate polarity into the reading. If it is a personal question, you will want to cut the cards toward you; cut them away from you if it is a question about someone other than yourself. Once the whole deck is back into your hand, deal from the top of the deck, placing the cards in the manner prescribed below.

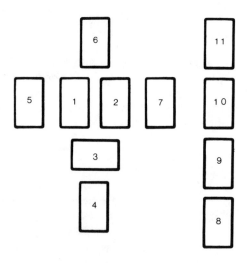

Meanings Of The Different Positions:

CARD 1: The significator or person involved in the reading.

CARD 2: The nature of the question asked.

CARD 3: The challenges or obstacles the person will have to deal with or overcome for a successful conclusion to the situation in question.

CARD 4: The foundation of the situation or what has already been experienced relative to the question.

CARD 5: What is behind the situation; forces that have been influential to the question, but are now passing from importance. The past.

CARD 6: What is pending in the situation. It may or may not occur. What is potential. Inspiration or assistance available.

CARD 7: What is about to unfold in the normal progression of events. The near future.

CARD 8: How the person asking the question is viewing the situation.

CARD 9: Feedback the person can expect from family and friends. Environmental influences. How others view the situation.

CARD 10: Mental attitudes that are influencing the situation; hopes and fears, anxiety and optimism.

CARD 11: Probable outcome, considered in context with the other cards. Remember, this is not a one-card reading; this card only has meaning in relevance to its relationship with all other cards of the spread.

The Relationship Spread

One of the areas most often asked about during a tarot reading is relationships. Will she? Does she? Does he still like me? Should we break up? Did we break up? These questions all involve two persons. So with these questions, it is helpful to lay down two sets of cards. One set is for the person asking the question, and these cards are dealt off the top of the deck. Another is for the person being asked about, and these cards are dealt off the bottom of the deck.

Since a relationship involves the interaction of two people, a relationship reading involves the interaction of two sets of cards. The reading shows how the two people are responding to each other at various levels of experience.

In this spread the reaction of the two individuals is clearly separated, allowing the reader to see how each partner responds independently *within* the relationship. This spread only shows how the individuals respond relative to this specific relationship.

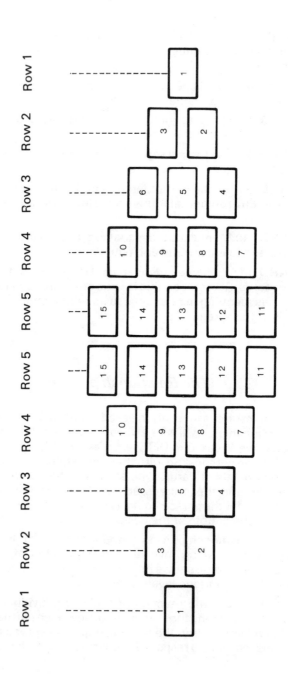

RELATIONSHIP SPREAD

Procedure:

Shuffle the cards as usual and concentrate on the relationship and on both of the people involved. After the cards are shuffled, cut into three piles and pick up the whole deck again. Deal the cards for each person in the manner prescribed below, remembering to use just the cards on the top of the deck for one person and just the ones on the bottom for the other person.

Meanings Of The Different Positions:

FIRST ROW: This card shows how each individual is approaching the relationship.

SECOND ROW: This row represents the mental image of the relationship. It describes the mental concept that each has of the relationship and the sort of mental rapport they perceive happening within the relationship.

THIRD ROW: This row represents the emotional involvement in the relationship. The center card is a balanced, consolidated representation of how each feels toward the other. The two outer cards represent the extremes of their feelings.

FOURTH ROW: This row shows how each fits into the structure of the other's life (the current reality of the relationship).

FIFTH ROW: This row is the element of time. The 11th and 12th cards represent the past. The 13th card represents the present, and the 14th and 15th cards represent the probable near future.

Interpretation:

Before beginning with the specific interpretation of each of the cards, look over all the cards laid out in front of you and see if the cards in each row seem to suggest harmony or if they are in a state of imbalance. Also look to see how the cards in the same position in each other's spreads correspond. Often there is a clue here about something one person is repeatedly doing to which the other person is reacting. The people in the relationship can make adjustments in either their awareness of each other's actions or the expression of their own actions.

Conclusion:

Learning the tarot doesn't require a good teacher, but it does require a good student. Time spent with the cards is mostly what it takes. If you wish ro read more on the subject, the following books cover a variety of levels.

Suggested Reading

Campbell, Joseph and Richard Roberts. *Tarot Revelations.*

Case, Paul Foster. *The Tarot.*
This book covers the major arcana. Deep and profound, this book needs to be read with concentration because of the abstract and esoteric interpretations of the cards. A valuable meditation guide.

Connoly, Eileen. *Tarot, A New Handbook for the Apprentice.*
Presented as a learning manual with exercises and step-by-step procedures, this is an excellent book for students. Advanced students can also benefit from the section on time and the tarot.

Crowley, Aleister. *The Book of Thoth.*
This is a companion book for the *Thoth Tarot Deck* by Crowley. Magical and esoteric in its language, it is best suited for those who appreciate Crowley's peculiarities. The section on the minor cards and meanings of the numbers can be helpful for all students.

Graves, R.D. *The Windows of the Tarot.*
This is an excellent source book for the Aquarian Tarot Deck, illustrated by Palladini. All illustrations are from the Aquarian Deck and the interpretations of the cards are clear and under-standable.

Waite, Arthur Edward. *The Pictorial Key to the Tarot.*
Waite writing on the Waite deck is certainly worth reading but one gets the feeling that he is, at times, purposely misleading and vague. This work contains divinatory meanings for each of the 78 cards.

3

I Ching

The week before our father died I was in Hawaii where I lived. I received a phone call from our sister saying that Dad was very ill and that if I wanted to see him before he died I should come to Seattle as soon as possible. I couldn't give an answer on the phone. I hung up feeling confused, disturbed, and frightened. I wondered if the family was overreacting. There had been other times when it seemed as if he would die, and he didn't. This could be another one of those times. Was the moment of death really at hand? I sat down and asked the I Ching about the state of Dad's health. I received Hexagram 28: Preponderance of the Great.

The hexagram talks about a Ridgepole that is thick and heavy in the middle, but weak on the ends. I realized right away that Dad was the Ridgepole. "This is a condition that cannot last; it must pass, or misfortune will result." This should have been the clue that his situation was bad and worsening, but in my inability to accept that he was dying, I misinterpreted it to mean that his illness was bad, but would quickly pass.

The hexagram goes on to say that the "load is too heavy for the strength of the supports." It seemed logical that the "supports" were the family. It looked as if everyone in the family would be emotionally pulled down by the situation, and I became even more afraid to go and be a part of that, especially if he really wasn't dying.

"It is an exceptional time and situation, therefore extraordinary measures are demanded. It is necessary to find a way of transition as quickly as possible and to take action." How much more clearly could it have told me about the state of affairs? But I didn't act. I sat and pondered.

Four days later, I received a call that he had died. I was hurt, stunned, and angry with myself. Why hadn't I responded when they first called? Why did I wait too long? I grabbed a few things and got on the next plane to Seattle. During the five-hour flight I re-read Hexagram 28 and realized that I was clearly told in advance of Dad's approaching death, but my own fears about the truth barred me from seeing the message.

...Lucy

As this story shows, the I Ching can be subtle, but it is not obscure. If you ask a question of the oracle and you receive an answer that you are not prepared to accept, your psyche will protect you by not comprehending the message. It is for this reason that we highly suggest your maintaining a personalized I Ching record or journal of all your questions and the hexagrams received. Date these, and later go back and fill in the data that in retrospect makes the hexagram more comprehendable. Through time, this journal will become a valuable teaching aid to self-discovery through the I Ching.

The I Ching's origins are firmly rooted in Eastern mysticism, it being considered the first and foremost of the Chinese classics. What becomes immediately apparent when you begin your work with the I Ching is that the good/bad, right/wrong dichotomy that is so prevalent in the western models is replaced with the Chinese concept of yin and yang which does not translate into the comfortable polarities we associate with answers. Yin and yang are seen as complementary forces that are present in all aspects of creation. They are two extremes of the ever-moving web of life.

The familiar symbol of this interaction shows the continual movement of one force transforming the other. Within the densest concentration of yin resides a seed for the yang and vice versa.

The yang is positive, active, light, and creative. The yin is yielding, passive, dark, and receptive. Their interaction is so deep that they depend on each other for existence; one is not possible without the other. The passive gives form to the active and the active animates the passive. It is the interaction of these two primal forces that creates the Tao (way) of life.

To study the I Ching is to come face-to-face with the Tao, which the life work and ultimate philosophy of the Chinese sage, Lao Tsu, so well exemplifies. The concept of Taoism will be best understood after reading the complete I Ching, from cover to cover. At that point it still remains difficult to reduce the concept into words, but you will have a feeling of the concept. The teaching has to do with moving in step with harmony itself, following the laws of nature, accepting change as a natural part of life, and moving with the grace of water. It has to do with accepting what is, and moving in accordance with that energy. The eastern approach is to adapt to this flow, in contrast to the western approach which is typified by attempting to change the flow.

This Taoist approach to life, the balancing of opposites, is found as a core teaching of the I Ching and also finds expression in T'ai Chi, Chinese medicine, calligraphy, and Chinese art. T'ai Chi is a moving yoga that helps the individual align with forces of yin and yang through body movement. Watching a skilled person perform the T'ai Chi movements can be an instructive aid in seeing the principles and polarity of the I Ching.

The I Ching teaches how to yield and adapt to the ever-changing nature of life. The cycles of when to act and when to wait will become more apparent with continual use of this oracle.

The I Ching is most helpful when you need to narrow your field of attention. This is opposed to the tarot, which is best suited for expanding your view by letting you know more about your options in a given situation.

Some understanding of the culture and traditions of classical Chinese history can be helpful as a way of learning even more from the teachings of the I Ching. If you already have empathy for early Chinese culture and the philosophy of Confucius and Lao Tsu, you will have no difficulty interpreting the images and applying these to your daily life. If this is an awkward or unfamiliar experience for you, you might prefer to use one of the more modern translations of the I Ching such as the *I Ching Workbook* by Wing.

The most respected, internationally acclaimed translation of the I Ching is the Wilhelm/Baynes edition which retains much of the flavor of the early Chinese culture. This translation will appear sexist to modern ears unless you understand the context from which it was written. The proper role for women at the time the book was written was that of subservience to men, and the Wilhelm translation reflects this attitude. You will need to take the time to translate the images into modern behavior. If you do not interpret the passages too literally you will quickly recognize that the Superior Man also represents the Superior Woman.

As you read the I Ching, particularly the Wilhelm translation, you will run across many references to Confucius. He is credited with adding personal commentaries to the original I Ching text. He appears to be one of the first to use the I Ching as a tool that went beyond political use, seeing it as a text and a credo of inner development on the journey toward peace and self-understanding.

Harmony and order are two of the main themes of Confucian philosophy. He believed that harmony was the natural state of affairs in the universe, and it was the human task to align with this harmony. This natural state of harmony in the cosmos was prefaced by first experiencing order within the state. For this to occur, the family needed to be in order, which could not occur unless the individuals who made up the family were in order. The system of order and harmony began within the individual, which extended to the family, then the state, and ultimately the cosmos.

Confucius saw in the I Ching a method for monitoring this balance of harmony. The I Ching could point to where personal adjustment was necessary to maintain harmony within the whole. The hexagrams address the various interactions between the four levels of harmony and direct attention to where it is most needed.

The concept of the four layers of harmony that the I Ching addresses has been a most helpful tool for me through the years. All of the oracles tend to answer the unasked question, and the I Ching does this in a most pinpointed way. There have been times when I've asked about a problem in my marriage and the I Ching clearly told me that the source of the problem was not in the relationship at all, but rather in my work. Other times, I have asked about a problem I was having at work and the I Ching pointed me toward an inner conflict that needed attention. The I Ching has taught me that the source of our problems and our knowledge of them are not always the same. We experience tension somewhere and tend to label it by whatever is conve-

nient and close at hand. The I Ching is wonderful for helping to identify the true source of the challenge that prompted a question.

...David

Confucius is known to have said that if he had another fifty years to live, he would devote this time to studying the I Ching, and in doing so, avoid great error and become without fault. What a tremendous testimony to the worth of this great book!

Legend has it, that in the year 3322 B.C., King Fu Hsi contemplated the ever-changing patterns in nature and noticed a harmony within the change. This was contrasted to the chaos and confusion of life within his kingdom. He is said to have developed the images of the trigrams from his observations of nature, and these were presented to his people as a model of how harmony operates within change.

He first named the polarity of heaven and earth yang and yin, respectively. As a visual image, the yang force was given the solid line ———. The yin force was given the broken line — —. From the four ways that these two forces of heaven and earth could come together, he saw the four seasons.

SUMMER   SPRING   AUTUMN   WINTER

Next he considered the human role in relation to heaven and earth and created a third line. The three lines could be combined in eight different ways, and this was the birth of the eight trigrams that form the basis of the I Ching.

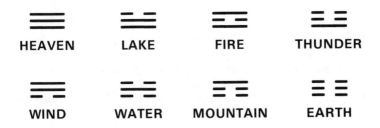

HEAVEN   LAKE   FIRE   THUNDER

WIND   WATER   MOUNTAIN   EARTH

The yin and the yang and the eight primary trigrams are the basic building blocks. It is possible to use the I Ching without familiarizing yourself with their meanings and attributes; you simply toss the coins and read the prescribed hexagram. However, if you wish to further your interpretative abilities, then contemplate on these images of nature. This will lead to a more personalized involvement with your readings.

As you read over these images of the Yin and the Yang, think of them as two extremes on the same pole.

YIN	**YANG**
yielding	firm
feminine	masculine
passive	assertive
dark	light
night	day
pause	act
non-action	action
receptive	creative
winter	summer
cold	hot
wet	dry
soft	hard
form	spirit

The following is a list of each of the trigrams and their corresponding meanings. Read each one of them and develop your own feelings about what it means to you. This will help you later in understanding the interpretations.

The Trigrams

≡ CH'IEN   Creative

This represents the positive, creative force of heaven. It symbolizes your own higher self. Its attributes are firmness, strength, and power. It is made up of all solid lines, representing its untiring power.

☱ TUI   Joyous

This is an image of a lake, with its strength, or mass, below and its openness above. It suggests the image of a mouth through which to express and/or receive. Its attributes are pleasure and joyousness. It can represent excess.

☲ LI   Fire

This trigram is drawn with its strong lines or strength on the outside and its weakness on the inside. It represents brightness and clarity. It is associated with fire. Attachments are also represented, serving as required fuel for the fire.

☳ CHEN   Thunder

With its strength below and passivity above, this trigram represents the arousing movement of power from within. Its attributes are movement and shock. There is restlessness and passion stirring from deep within to upset the peace on the surface.

☷ K'UN   Receptive

The image is that of earth: passive, yielding, submissive, and nurturing. The trigram is drawn with all yielding lines, representing its greatest strength. Opposite to The Creative and responsive to it, it represents the physical part of nature and The Creative represents the spiritual. It receives the creative energy of Heaven, giving it form and substance through devotion.

☶ KEN   Mountain

Strong on the surface and passive below is the image. Its attributes are tranquility and calmness, as it suggests keeping still and resting. It can also represent an obstacle and thus a situation of being forced to keep still and wait.

☵ K'AN   Water

The passive lines are on the outside and the strength lies within. Passive and yielding to external forces, it always maintains its essential identity. Like water, it represents the mysterious, the deep, the profound. Also known as The Abysmal, it can represent danger, peril, and difficulty.

☴ SUN   Wind

The strong lines are above and the weak is below. The message is one of the proper attitude in disseminating information: remain strong in your intent, yet be receptive to feedback. The image of the wind is penetrating, pervasive and influential. This is the gentle wind that touches all but can become scattered unless it is focused. This trigram represents insights as well as indecisiveness.

Definitions of Terms Used Throughout the I Ching

BOOK OF CHANGE: The I Ching

BROKEN LINE: A passive, yin line. Can be a 6 or an 8. (See section on procedure.)

COINS: Popular method of consulting the I Ching.

CROSS THE GREAT RIVER: The challenge or task at hand needs to be forged. Move forward. Possible journey.

DANGER: Time to exercise great caution.

FIRM: Solid, unchanging.

GREAT MAN: Someone in authority, either sex.

HEXAGRAM: 2 trigrams, one above the other.

HUMILIATION: Strong embarassment. Proposed action will lower self esteem.

I CHING: Book of Change. Oracle.

MOVING LINE: All heads or all tails. Can be a 6 or a 9. Line in the process of change.

NO BLAME: Regardless of the outcome, it is beyond your control and there is nothing you can do. You will not be held responsible.

PERSEVERANCE BRINGS HUMILIATION: The only safe course is to give up your plan altogether.

PERSEVERANCE FURTHERS: Persist with your plans.

REGRET: There will be regret if you persist.

REMORSE: You will later feel guilt and wish you had acted otherwise.

SOLID LINE: An assertive, yang line. Can be a 7 or a 9.

SUBLIME SUCCESS: Complete success.

SUPERIOR MAN: His conduct is always given as the standard one should follow to achieve success.

TAO: Path of harmony. Path of least resistance.

TRIGRAM: Group of 3 lines.

UNDERTAKE SOMETHING: Make a definite plan.

YANG: Solid, masculine, assertive. Can be a 7 or 9 line.

YIELD: Feminine, dark, passive. A broken line. Can be a 6 or an 8.

YARROW STALKS: Traditional method of I Ching consultation.

Asking Questions Of The Oracle

When asking a question of the I Ching, it is as if you were stopping time and observing your position within your particular cycle of experience. Is the experience growing or waning in intensity? What can you expect if you continue on the same path... more of the same, or is the situation about to change into something else? Using the I Ching becomes a way of decoding the mystery of the future by allowing a closer look into the present conditions.

The most difficult concept for most Westerners to grasp is that change cannot be controlled by going against it or in any way resisting it. If the change is going to occur, then it is not resistance, but adaptation that will best serve your needs. An obvious example is the changing seasons and how you must adapt your clothes, activities and awareness to be in harmony with the times. The I Ching teaches this path of adaptation.

Approach the I Ching as if it were a person, a wise friend, that you are consulting for advice. A dialogue will naturally occur. You will begin to turn to the I Ching, with time and practice, as you would to a well-trusted friend. Acquaint yourself with the terminology and the concepts of yin, yang, and the Tao. Once you are familiar with these, the I Ching will be more meaningful, and you can devote your attention to the teachings you are receiving rather than the process of getting there. The terminology does need to be personally translated so that you can apply the situation in the hexagram to your life. Don't neglect your interpretive ability once you are familiar with the routines and the language. Spend time meditating on the images as you understand them, and you will get the added personal meaning that you are seeking. Your intuition will help you in this process.

Consultation Of The I Ching

NECESSARY TOOLS:
1. A copy of the I Ching. There are many translations available, so before you purchase your copy, you should spend time looking over the different presentations. We highly recommend *I CHING, BOOK OF CHANGES* by Wilhelm/Baynes; *THE I CHING WORKBOOK* by Wing; or *A TRAVELER'S BOOK OF CHANGES* by Jade Easter (See Suggested Reading for other texts.)

2. Three coins of the same size. These can be three pennies, or three dimes, or three Chinese coins. Alternatively, a set of yarrow stalks might be used. However, this method is more complicated and will be presented at the end of the chapter.

3. A quiet place where you can formulate your question, consult the I Ching, and meditate on your hexagram.

4. A notebook in which to record your question, the hexagram received, and comments on the outcome after the situation has passed.

PROCEDURE FOR CONSULTATION:

1. Define The Question. As with most forms of divination, this is often the step that takes the longest. When the question comes to you, write it in your notebook as succinctly as possible. Now ponder the question, and check each one of the words to see that they are the specific words to best define the intent of your question.

One technique of thoroughly understanding your question is to repeat the question. Each time emphasize a different word, checking that each word is the exact one for your question. If your question is "Should I pursue my relationship with Bob?", then on the first repetition you would emphasize the word *should*, the next time *I*, the next time *pursue*, etc.

2. Approach The Oracle Positively. To receive affirmative, growth-oriented responses from your inquiries you must be in a corresponding frame of mind. Know that it will give you the information you seek. If you need an answer fast, the I Ching is not the oracle to use. When you ask a question, be prepared to spend time with the process and to follow the advice that is given. Another rule that applies to all oracles is that you only ask the question once.

3. Approach The Oracle In Meditation. Quiet yourself, and rid your mind of all chatterings, anxieties, and possible projections.

4. Throw The Coins. Meditate on the question and drop the three coins simultaneously. The first throw will be recorded on the bottom line. The next throw will be recorded on the line right above that. Continue in this manner up to the top, or the 6th line.

5. Record The Numerical Value Of The Coins. Give each head a value of 2 and each tail a value of 3. There are four possible combinations of heads and tails with three coins. Thus, the total value of the three coins, in any combination, can amount to 6, 7, 8, or 9. Using the following conversion table, you record either a yin line or a yang line for each toss.

All broken lines are yin and passive. All solid lines are yang and assertive.

6 __x__   #3 heads ... Changing Yin
7 _____   #2 heads + 1 tail ... Stable Yang
8 __ __   #1 heads + 2 tails ... Stable Yin
9 __o__   #3 tails ... Changing Yang

6 and 9 are called *moving lines*, and to remind yourself that they are in the process of change, they have an X or an O placed over the lines. Moving lines have a special significance and are interpreted separately. In the text, following the interpretation of each hexagram is a section that is devoted to the moving lines. Not all of your hexagrams will include moving lines.

Record In This Manner:

	_____	top or line 6
Upper trigram	_____	line 5
	_____	line 4
		HEXAGRAM
	_____	line 3
Lower trigram	_____	line 2
	_____	line 1

6. Locate Your Hexagram. Now that you have thrown the coins and have 6 lines in front of you, an upper and a lower trigram, it is time to find the numerical correspondence of your 6 lines, or hexagram. The last page of the Wilhelm/Baynes translation has a reference guide to the hexagrams. If you are using another translation, it might be in the front or the back of the book, but it is there. All guides or grids are used in the same manner. Locate the lower trigram on the left column and locate your upper trigram on the top of the grid.

By following down vertically from your upper trigram and across horizontally from your lower trigram to the point where the two join, you will converge with the number of your hexagram. Record this number next to your 6 lines or hexagram.

UPPER TRIGRAM / LOWER TRIGRAM	CH'IEN ☰	CHEN ☳	K'AN ☵	KEN ☶	K'UN ☷	SUN ☴	LI ☲	TUI ☱
CH'IEN ☰	1	34	5	26	11	9	14	43
CHEN ☳	25	51	3	27	24	42	21	17
K'AN ☵	6	40	29	4	7	59	64	47
KEN ☶	33	62	39	52	15	53	56	31
K'UN ☷	12	16	8	23	2	20	35	45
SUN ☴	44	32	48	18	46	57	50	28
LI ☲	13	55	63	22	36	37	30	49
TUI ☱	10	54	60	41	19	61	38	58

EXAMPLE: Say that after tossing the coins, you created a hexagram that looked like this:

Use the top, horizontal row to locate the pattern of the top 3 lines of your hexagram. Use the vertical row on the side to locate the pattern of the bottom 3 rows of your hexagram. Where these two rows intersect is the number of your hexagram. In this example,

on top and

on the bottom is hexagram #31.

7. Interpret Your Hexagram. If you are using the Wilhelm/Baynes translation, you may find the language somewhat intellectual and pendantic. Keep in mind that the original I Ching was written for the ruling class of China, and much of the advice concerns how to remain in power and how to follow the etiquette of a ruling class. This can seem formal and at times obtuse. This is probably the reason for the proliferation of new translations that speak in a more modern tone. Whichever translation you are using, you must now make the transition from the words in the text to your own life situation. This is a key step to unlocking the mystery. Intuition will be more significant in the interpretation than the intellect, so move slowly over the words and images.

8. Changing Lines. If your hexagram contains no changing lines, the situation is said to be stable. If your hexagram contains changing lines, either 6's or 9's, then you must construct a second hexagram with the changing lines changed to their opposite.

EXAMPLE:

Hexagram #5   Hexagram #61

Visualize the image of a pendulum swinging from one extreme to the other. Throwing 3 heads or 3 tails means that the pendulum has swung as far as it can in one direction, and now begins to move in the opposite direction. A 9 changes into an 8, and a 6 changes into a 7. The changing yang line becomes yin, and the changing yin line becomes yang. Once you have constructed your new hexagram with the changing lines, turn to the grid and find the number that corresponds to your upper and lower trigram.

The first hexagram will depict the situation as it now stands, and the second will represent the situation after the changes that are indicated have taken place. The changing lines themselves are significant, and there is a passage following the interpretation of the first hexagram that will deal with each changing line separately. Read these carefully. Remember to read only the lines that were changing in your original hexagram.

Through carefully following the above eight steps, you should now be at a point of intensified awareness concerning your question.

The Yarrow Stalk Method

This is another method for obtaining hexagrams. Because it is much more complicated and takes considerably more time, it is often forsaken for the more expedient method of throwing the coins. From the gathering and preparing of your stalks to the added time spent with your question, this method will bring you closer to your question than using the coins. We have found that by spending as much time focusing on the question as this method requires, the answer to the question is often known to you before you read it.

SELECTING YOUR STALKS: Yarrow grows in most parts of the country as a wild herb. Find a patch of it in your area and watch it grow. In the fall, when the flower has died, it is time to collect your stalks. You will need fifty stalks approximately nine inches in length. Select stalks that have a uniform diameter and a nine-inch section of straight stalk. Cut your nine-inch segments and place them in the sun to dry. After they are dried, gather them together and tie them into a bundle. Store them with your I Ching in a safe place.

PROCEDURE: Follow the same procedure for defining the question and approaching the oracle positively as with the coin method.

STEP 1. Take your bundle of fifty stalks and hold them as you meditate on the question.

STEP 2. Separate one stalk from the bundle and place it aside from the others. This stalk remains apart during the entire process.

STEP 3. Separate the bundle into two piles. Place one pile on your left and one pile on your right.

STEP 4. Take one stalk from the right-hand pile and place it between the last two fingers on your left hand.

STEP 5. Reduce the pile on the left side by groups of fours until the pile has 1, 2, 3 or 4 stalks left.

STEP 6. Pick up the remaining 1 to 4 stalks and place them between the ring and middle fingers of the left hand.

STEP 7. Reduce the pile on the right side by groups of fours until there are between 1 and 4 stalks left.

STEP 8. Pick up the remaining 1 to 4 stalks and add them to the stalks you have been saving in your left hand. You will now have a total of either 5 or 9 stalks in your left hand. Set these aside.

STEP 9. Gather the remaining stalks and refocus on your

question. As you do, again divide the stalks into two piles as before.

STEP 10. Repeat steps 4 through 8 with your newly divided piles.

STEP 11. Gather the reamining stalks after the reduction process. You will have either 4 or 8 stalks. Set these aside.

STEP 12. Gather the remaining stalks. Focus on your question. Separate them into two piles as before and reduce them by fours through the same procedure. The process will once again lead you to 4 or 8 stalks and these are also set aside.

STEP 13. With the three piles you have set aside, use the table below to determine the line you have cast.

Number Of Stalks:

Set Aside	Type Of Line	Notation	Numerical Value
5 + 4 + 4	Changing Yang	———	9
9 + 8 + 8	Changing Yin	— —	6
5 + 8 + 8 or 9 + 8 + 4 or 9 + 4 + 8	Stable Yang	———	7
5 + 4 + 8 or 5 + 8 + 4 or 9 + 4 + 4	Stable Yin	— —	8

You have now created your first line. Repeat this process for each of the six lines of the hexagram.

This chapter on the I Ching has been a brief introduction to the topic. It is designed to give you the necessary information to begin using it as a divinatory tool. It is experience that will be your greatest teacher concerning its usefulness in your life. If you wish to further your studies there is a wealth of information available.

Suggested Reading

Blofield, J. *The Book of Change*.

Dhiegh, Khigh Alx. *The Eleventh Wing*.

Easter, Jade. *A Traveler's Book of Changes*.
This is an abbreviated translation that has been condensed to essential keywords. It comes in a pocket-size version that is an excellent traveling companion for those familiar with the I Ching.

Legge, James. *The I Ching*.

Tsu, Lao. *Tao Te Ching*.
A poetic book outlining the precepts of Taoism. Although not directly connected to the I Ching, this is a companion study that can be most beneficial for understanding the spirit behind the I Ching.

Wilhelm, Hellmut. *Heaven, Earth, and Man in the Book of Changes*.

Wilhelm, Hellmut. *Change, Eight Lectures on the I Ching*.

The philosophy, history, and key principles are presented in such a way that serious students can deepen their understanding of the I Ching.

Wilhelm, Richard. *The I Ching*.

The definitive I Ching. A scholarly presentation. For serious students, it is a must. This translation retains the flavor of classical Chinese culture and is the clearest presentation of the philosophy of the I Ching.

Wing, R.L. *The I Ching Workbook*.

This is an excellent modern translation. The formal language of the Wilhelm edition is translated into modern language, and Wing does a fine job of applying the hexagrams to modern life.

4

Numerology

Of all the systems you will study, numerology will be the easiest to learn, and the one you can most quickly facilitate. There is nothing esoteric about your age, birthdate, street address, telephone number, parking stall number....or is there? Hidden within each of these numbers that make up your everyday world, there is a symbol with a message. Sound like a "fortune cookie"....break it open and read the message? It is. Everything that you do or touch that involves numbers holds a message.

When I was first introduced to numerology, I dropped everything I was doing and became absorbed into the romance of numbers. They are so simple, yet so profound. I became curious and fascinated with the numbers of my life. People, places and words themselves were the subject matter and the more I studied, the more my knowledge grew concerning these parts of my life. Decoding these symbols was adding insight and depth to my everyday world.

...Lucy

Numerology is a method of organizing a perspective as to where you have been and where you are going. It is a way to segment life in an orderly fashion.

Numbers themselves can not make anything happen in your life. All things in the material world resonate at a specific level and numbers and letters are representations of the vibrational patterns. Numbers are a convenience of language and are abstract qualities which only refer to real things; they are not the things themselves. The most numerology can do for you is describe points within a cycle and offer a method of interpreting and utilizing these points. It provides a structure for understanding life.

By applying your understanding of numbers, you will become aware of some of the rhythms and cycles in your life. You will start to notice when it is best for you to act and when it is best to wait. Through numerology, you will have an opportunity to look within yourself with more awareness.

Numerology is also one of the basic factors in the study of astrology and tarot and will aid you in the interpretation of both these studies.

****

BASIC RULE: There is a fundamental numerical manipulation that you should understand before going any farther. Whenever you look at a series of numbers, always add them horizontally. If this final product has more than two digits, add them horizontally again until you have produced a single digit.

EXAMPLE: Your address is 844. Add the numbers horizontally like this: $8 + 4 + 4 = 16$. 16 is not a single digit, so continue to add: $1 + 6 = 7$. 7 is a single digit, so we consider that to be the number which represents your home.

ANOTHER EXAMPLE: Your birthdate is September 2, 1919. Begin by adding month, day, and year: $9 + 2 + 1 + 9 + 1 + 9 = 31$. Once again, 31 is not a single digit, so add the two digits to reduce the number to one digit: $3 + 1 = 4$. The number which represents your birthdate is 4.

Necessary Tools

I. The following table of correspondences is necessary for reducing names to their numeric equivalents.

TABLE OF CORRESPONDENCES

1	2	3	4	5	6	7	8	9
A	B	C	D	E	F	G	H	I
J	K	L	M	N	O	P	Q	R
S	T	U	V	W	X	Y	Z	

II. You will need an understanding of the INTRINSIC MEANINGS of each of the numbers.

III. You will need an OPEN MIND so that you can truly observe numbers at work. As you study numbers, watch yourself and those around you. Look at your own life in retrospect and see if the personal year numbers were accurate symbols for what you experienced during those years. Remember, you are the laboratory where these experiments in validity are taking place.

IV. Keep a special NOTEBOOK for numerology and record all personal observations. In this you should keep all copies of the numerology you do for family and friends. Your notebook will become your best reference book.

V. PATIENCE. Your observations can only be meaningful if they are done with accuracy. Take the time to add and record correctly.

Definition of Terms

LIFE PATH: Add together day + month + year of birth. This represents the typical way you approach life experiences.

UNIVERSAL YEAR: Add together the digits that make up the current year. This represents the trends and challenges that are affecting everyone in a given year.

PERSONAL YEAR: Add together month of birth + day of birth + current year. This represents your personal lessons and opportunities for the year.

INNER PERSONALITY: Add together the number equivalents of the vowels that make up your complete given name. This represents the private or concealed side of yourself.

OUTER PERSONALITY: Add together the number equivalents of the consonants that make up your complete given name. This represents your personality, the social you.

DESTINY NUMBER: Add together the numbers that make up your complete given name (add together your inner and outer personality numbers). This represents the role you may potentially play in society depending on your ability to harmonize your inner and outer personalities.

MASTER NUMBERS: Numbers 11 and 22 are the only ones that you will work with in this beginning guide to numerology.

When reducing your numbers to a single digit, always note when the next-to-the-last reduction produces either a number 11 and/or 22, and take special note of them before you reduce them to a number 2 or 4. These numbers offer more opportunity for expression than the other numbers and also demand more from the individual. It can also be said that they carry more social responsibility.

Meaning of the Numbers

Numbers represent one of the simplest and easiest cycles that you will learn about. They are symbols for a cycle that is recurring and can be seen as stages in an evolutionary process. Learn the numbers and remember them as markers in the complete cycle. See them as growing out of the preceding number and developing into the next number.

Keywords for the Numbers

No.	Keywords	Actor	Planet
1	Beginning, initiation, leadership	The Leader	Sun
2	Reflection, opposition, duality, balance	The Nurturer	Moon
3	Expansion, growth, enthusiasm, advancement	The Explorer	Jupiter
4	Structure, foundation, form, realization	The Worker	Saturn
5	Uncertainty, realignment, flux, change	The Student	Mercury
6	Harmony, balance, appreciation, indulgence	The Peacemaker	Venus
7	Intuition, aloofness, rebellion, inner awareness	The Eccentric	Uranus
8	Power, organization, enterprise, control	The Executive	Mars
9	Wisdom, understanding, transition, service	The Mystic	Neptune

10	Completion, rebirth, transformation	.... The Reborn .... Pluto
11	Idealism, inspiration, vision	...... The Visionary
22	Planning, engineering, humanitarianism	..... The Manifestor

Descriptive Numerology

Descriptive numerology works with "the givens" of your life: your date of birth and name as they appear on your birth certificate. These remain with you always and are interpreted as the foundation from which you grow. You may change your name through marriage, spiritual commitment, or choice, but the name you were given at birth is the one that forms your personal foundation of life.

There are four main tools for describing the different aspects of yourself:

I. LIFE PATH, based on the date of birth.
II. INNER PERSONALITY, based on the vowels in your name.
III. OUTER PERSONALITY, based on the consonants in your name.
IV. DESTINY NUMBER, based on the combined vowels and consonants in your name.

LIFE PATH: This number corresponds with the general way you approach life situations. It also describes your special innate abilities.

The Life Path number is found by adding together each of the digits of your birthday, and then reducing them by addition until you get a single digit or one of the Master Numbers.

RULE: Month + Day + Year of Birth = LIFE PATH NUMBER
EXAMPLE:

Birthdate of December 4, 1948.
12 + 4 + 1948   1 + 2 + 4 + 1 + 9 + 4 + 8 = 29
Next, Reduce 29 by addition: 2 + 9 = 11
The Life Path number for this birthday is the Master Number 11.

EXAMPLE:

Birthday of July 27, 1951.
7 + 2 + 7 + 1 + 9 + 5 + 1 = 32

Reduce 32: 3 + 2 = 5
Life Path number = 5

Following is a list of the meanings of each of the Life Path numbers:

LIFE PATH #1: You are a leader and an initiator. The best in life comes to you when you accept roles of responsibility and authority. Strength and individuality are your trademarks; others have always seen it, and you wear it well when you choose to display it. Be confident, original and willing to stand alone if you have to.

You should not accept compromise in pursuing your direction in life, however, if this non-compromising attitude carries over to social interactions, you will alienate others through over-aggressiveness. You will be Number 1 at something in your life. Express yourself with pride, flair, and courage. These attributes will help give you confidence in yourself.

Your greatest obstacle is that of being too arrogant and self-centered, leaving no room in your life for anyone other than an appreciative audience.

LIFE PATH #2: Relationships are the key to your life. You are not interested in living your life alone, only in sharing it with a partner. You make an excellent worker because of your willingness to accept guidance and your eagerness to please. You are quite willing to protect and sustain loved ones. You respond to the needs of the moment. You are resilient to the point of being able to pull through the worst of any crisis. You are willing to cooperate and share in a relationship, but you expect results and equality.

Your challenge is one of learning how to incorporate the opinions of others without giving up personal integrity. Express your feelings as they come up. You are moody and need to occasionally remind yourself to let go of the past and move on.

LIFE PATH #3: You are the communicator, the optimist, and the proverbial student of life. Self-expression is your key to happiness. New projects excite and grab your attention. When you are excited, that energy easily spills over to those with whom you come in contact. Watch that you don't spread yourself too thin with all of your varied interests. You are versatile, easily excitable, and the person who always wants MORE from life. Because you are adaptable and generally fun to be with, you are often found among a group of friends. You are popular and defined as inspirational. Your versatility is a talent that should be utilized through your work.

Watch out for being a dilettante. Learn to put depth into your studies. Your test is one of finishing at least a portion of the projects you begin without stretching yourself to the breaking point. The phrase "too many irons in the fire," was probably inspired by the actions of a number 3. Your desire is to grow, expand, learn, teach, and to be more than you were in your past.

LIFE PATH #4: A hard worker with a highly developed sense of responsibility, you are the solid individual whose work can benefit an entire community. Life doesn't seem to come easy for you, but this is a source of strength. What you have is what you have created for yourself. It could be said that you thrive on adversity, but wanting to work for what you get is closer to the truth. You will only accept that which you have earned, and you are not seeking a "free ride" in any area of your life. You are organized, hard-working, steady, and willing to follow the necessary routines to accomplish goals. You have an excellent ability to concentrate and the tenacity not to give up on a project until it is completed.

Your inner growth and development are more important to you than what you are doing with your outer, social life. Your life has been marked by struggle, but patience, devotion, and endurance will be the keynotes to your success. Avoid becoming stoic and rigid.

LIFE PATH #5: You are bright, clever, alert, and the most versatile of the numbers. There is a rapid and continual turnover in the events of your life which has forced you to develop your keen sense of adaptability. You crave new experiences and bore easily with routines. You are a natural at any type of communication and could easily be found in a profession of writing, speaking, or sales. It is the breadth of experience which you have accumulated that makes you fascinating in the eyes of others. Watch leaving a trail of unfinished projects and incomplete relationships in your wake.

Your challenge is to tame your fickle nature and recognize and sustain that which is valuable in your life. Adding depth to your involvements and adventures can offer more fulfillment to your life.

LIFE PATH #6: You know how to enjoy the good things in life, and are known for your cultured taste. You exhibit refinement and style in your speech, your dress, and in your home surroundings. Justice, balance, and harmony are the crucial elements of your expression. You have an excellent feel for colors and appreciation for both art and music. Strong family ties offer cohesiveness and meaning to your life. Quality time with a few select friends in your own home is a favorite pastime.

Your main challenge is that of learning the flexibility that true sharing requires. Once you accept situations and relationships exactly as they are, without trying to make any improvements, you become happier. Yes, you need to defend and protect that which you value, but you must periodically review your values to see if they are consistent with your life goals.

LIFE PATH #7: You are eccentric, unusual, aloof, but amazingly friendly. Even as a child, you valued your privacy, a quality that remains with you throughout your life. You are a dreamer, idealistic, mystical and always a philosopher. No one really knows what is going on inside of you as you are not the type to share your secrets. Meditation and quiet time are essential if you are to understand the deeper mysteries of life and the internal questions that plague you. It is through these that you preserve your individuality as the key to happiness and fulfillment. There are many times when you will feel like a misfit in the world, which may be because you are searching for more meaning to life than others or simply rebel against being one of the ordinary.

Your challenge is one of developing warmth and emotional intimacy with your loved ones. You are unusually bright, intelligent, and perceptive. You are often misunderstood by those who claim to know you best. Freedom is your ticket to happiness.

LIFE PATH #8: You are efficient, organized, and a hard worker. Serious and goal-minded, you can be depended upon to carry through with obligations. Your tendency is to take on more and more responsibility. Use your ability to delegate authority to keep from becoming over-burdened. Your excellent managerial skills and your drive for success and control will place you at the top of your chosen profession. You can become fascinated with your own power and will be attracted to others of great power. For maximum growth you must remain humble and thankful for the respect and trust that others place in you.

Your challenge is one of right use of power. Be aware of what you are willing to sacrifice to get to the top. Leadership and success are yours when you harness and temper your tremendous drive for achievement and recognition. It will be yours if you are patient and understanding of the real responsibility of being able to exert your will over others.

LIFE PATH #9: You are the dreamer, the artist, the genius, and, at times, the martyr. Yours is a path of empathy for the misunderstood. You have experienced much confusion in establishing a foundation for your life. It is the school of life that has offered you your greatest education. Your keen perception allows you to immediately see through phonies and pierce facades, as you are seeking contact with the real essence of life. Being the most complex of the numbers you are difficult to understand because of the depth of your sensitivity and awareness.

You are compassionate and extremely sensitive to your emotional environment which causes extreme shifts in your moods. Fulfillment comes from being needed, appreciated, and being involved in some sort of service. You have deep, intense, but often short-lived involvements. You do your work....then move on. Yours is a life of extremes, and you are known for your sensitivity and caring.

LIFE PATH #11: As the first of the Master Numbers, you are the Master Student, the idealist who is on a quest for meaning. A seeker of truth, you are willing to jump into any class, teaching, or walk of life that offers potential hope and insight. Others look to you for guidance and you are a natural instructor. There are times when your enthusiasm borders on fanaticism and becomes tiring, but listening to your keen intuition can thwart problems in this area. The life you lead will be the ultimate teaching you impart to the world.

Number 11 also reduces to a number 2, and 11s must learn the lessons of cooperation before they can serve as a voice of inspiration for others. It is the special task of 11s to keep the dreams, visions, and hopes of others alive.

LIFE PATH #22: This is the number of the Master Teacher. Being knowledgeable in the ways of the world will create a responsibility to pass learned information onto others. The number 11 holds the vision, and the number 22 holds the practical key in applying this wisdom for the betterment of humanity. A concern for the welfare of mankind will lead to a teaching of universal concepts.

Your challenge is to maintain the strength of character needed to be the voice of discrimination and leadership. 22 reduces to a #4, and all of the lessons of perseverance must be learned before the qualities of leadership begin to surface in your life.

REMINDER: Your Life Path number remains with you throughout life because it is derived from your birthdate, which never changes. You will face different aspects of your particular Life Path at different times, but the underlying lesson will remain the same. The positive aspects of your number are the skills and abilities you should be utilizing, as they indicate your special gifts and talents. The negative aspects of the Life Path number are characteristics you must learn to balance.

Your Destiny Number

For this section, it is important to use the complete name that you were given at birth, even if you no longer go by that name. The given name is representative of the universal response to your arrival in life before you began your personal individuation process. Nicknames, pet names, and changed names all apply to the predictive aspect of numerology that will be dealt with later in this chapter.

Your Destiny Number is made up of two separate parts, the Inner Personality and the Outer Personality.

Inner Personality

In some books, this is referred to as the "heart's desire" or the "soul urge." This number represents the concealed side of yourself. It rules your secret ambitions and desires. Others see this quality only after spending much close time with you; these are the qualities of your most private self. The number of your Inner Personality offers clues as to your calling for personal creative expression. Everyone has a creative calling, but not all are responding to it. Are you giving this side of yourself the attention that it needs?

RULES: Add up all the vowels (a, e, i, o, u, and y when it is used as a vowel) in your name and reduce them to a single digit or one of the Master Numbers. Refer to the TABLE OF CORRESPOND-ENCES at the beginning of the chapter for the number equivalents of the letters.

EXAMPLE:

    1 9   5 6   5   6   1 + 9 + 5 + 6 + 5 + 6 = 32   3 + 2 = 5
    DAVID GEORGE POND

    3 7 5 5 7   6   3 + 7 + 5 + 5 + 7 + 6 = 33   3 + 3 = 6
    LUCY EVELYN POND

Figure out your Inner Personality and see if it reveals more about the side of your desires and expression than what is shown to the outside world.

Descriptions For The Inner Personality Types:

INNER #1: You see yourself as an initiator, a leader, an investigator, and a spokesperson. You always put yourself in the center of activities. Regardless of how outwardly yielding you may appear, you never back down from a confrontation. Secretly desiring control and power, you want to move to the top or into the limelight whenever possible. You are not an easy person to work with as you do not accept orders well, secretly wanting your own way.

Your strength is in your ability to be your own authority and pursue life exactly as you desire. This gives you an inner strength that is of tremendous benefit.

INNER #2: You see yourself as a follower rather than a leader, and smooth relationships are a high priority. You enjoy helping others and being involved in cooperative efforts, but secretly you may lack the confidence to complete a project alone. With an inner nature that is sweet, compassionate, and loving, you rarely offend others. You consider yourself sensitive and perhaps even an artist who dislikes physical work. Your refined nature allows you to mix well in divergent social groups.

INNER #3: You are the optimist with the ultimate positive approach to life. A creative self-identity gives you the confidence to do anything you choose. At heart, you are the romantic who is seeking joy and happiness mixed with some high adventure. Follow your dreams and fantasies and always do things with grandiose style. Impatient with pessimism, you become frustrated with those who think small and try to scale down ideas.

INNER #4: Security is of the utmost importance to you. Organized, practical, and even methodical in your thinking and planning, you believe this is the way to achieve desired success. Seeing yourself as reliable, loyal, and dependable, you secretly desire recognition for the work you have done that all too often goes unnoticed. As the practical realist who believes that nothing is earned without hard work, you become suspicious about that which comes too easily.

INNER #5: You define yourself as adventuresome and experimental. Being a fun-loving person by nature, you enjoy the company of a broad spectrum of people. Regardless of what you say, deep inside you see all commitments lasting only as long as they hold your attention. Your secret desire is to do whatever you want, whenever you want. You desire to experience the variety of life. You have a strong need to be in the flow of communication and to exercise your speaking and writing skills.

INNER #6: You define yourself as a domestic personality who places home and family above all other considerations. Seeing yourself as the one who brings harmony and beauty into your personal environment, you secretly wish others could be as enjoyable to be around as you. Your social time is invested in family and loved ones with little interest in hobnobbing with those you don't know intimately. You consider yourself to be just and fair in all your relationships.

INNER #7: You see yourself as unique, unusual, eccentric, and misunderstood by those around you. You feel troubled by the noise of the world and want to escape it. Aloneness offers a vantage point to observe the curiosities of life. You love to analyze, are intensely secretive, and desire more privacy. You secretly define yourself as a mystic and a philosopher.

INNER #8: You define yourself as a good manager and an excellent organizer. There is no doubt in your mind as to whether or not you are important...you are. Seeing yourself as capable of any amount of responsibility, usually you are "too busy" to let go and have fun. Your secret desire for more power is fueled by an inner need to control situations.

INNER #9: You see yourself as a continual source of compassion, understanding, and sympathy for others. You are the silent sufferer who gives totally of yourself. You feel wise in the ways of the world and desire to share this wisdom with others. You are always there when someone needs you.

INNER #11: You know that you are intuitive with psychic hunches that continually prove to be correct. Your sensitivity is unique, bordering on clairvoyance. It seems that you are asked to endure more emotional ups and downs than most, but you have the strength and stamina to rebound from any disruption. You secretly desire more recognition for the work you accomplish.

INNER #22: You define yourself as a chosen planner with an inner responsibility to a futuristic environment. You have an excellent ability to organize and stay with a goal until it is achieved. You are the Master Planner and you know it. You know that you will leave this earth having amassed material security.

Your Outer Personality

This is the part of your personality that is most obvious to others. It represents how others view you and is not necessarily the real you. This is what others remember after the first acquaintance. It is the face you present to the world. Knowing more about your Outer Personality can help you make the best impression when meeting others; it offers clues as to your characteristic habits and mannerisms. Take the time to become more aware of these traits and ask yourself if there are some changes or improvements you would like to make in yourself.

RULES: Add up all the consonants in your full name and then reduce these to either a single digit or one of the Master Numbers.

EXAMPLE:

DAVID GEORGE POND
4 4 4   7   9 7   7 5 4
$4 + 4 + 4 + 7 + 9 + 7 + 7 + 5 + 4 = 51$ $5 + 1 = 6$

LUCY EVELYN POND
3 3   4 3 5 7 5 4
$3 + 3 + 4 + 3 + 5 + 7 + 5 + 4 = 34$ $3 + 4 = 7$

Figure out your Outer Personality number and learn more about how you are seen by others. Follow the example above and use the Table of Correspondences at the beginning of the chapter.

Descriptions for the Outer Personality types:

OUTER #1: You appear totally self-confident and self-reliant, and perhaps this is why others look to you for guidance. You are highly original, courageous, unique, and comfortable standing out in a crowd. It appears that you need no one; even those closest to you do not feel that they are essential in your life. You can be aggressive with a tendency to dominate social situations. You need a clear-cut purpose to remain involved in anything.

OUTER #2: You appear artistic, diplomatic, and reserved. Judging from first appearances, you prefer a quiet and calm social atmosphere. You are seen as fussy, even critical over details. You are considered a good companion, especially with the opposite sex. You are charming, and at times cunning. You seem uncomfortable when you are asked to stand alone, even for a short time.

OUTER #3: You appear to be the perfect dilettante, trying a hand at all the various forms of creative self-expression. You are the enthusiast and the eternal optimist, adding a positive note to any group. Others define you as "lucky;" they even think that you have some sort of guardian angel hovering over you. Known as both charming and witty, you are excellent with words.

OUTER #4: You appear reliable, honest, and hard-working; people immediately trust you. Known for your practical approach to life, you carry a conservative reputation. Others see you as responsible but shy and reserved. It appears to be difficult for you to enjoy luxury and the frivolity in life.

OUTER #:5: You appear the playful flirt, exuberant and outgoing. You seem to live completely in the moment; there appears to be no past or future in your concerns. Is it true that no one can pin you down? At a party you talk to everyone, but none feel they've had a conversation with you. You are the dreamer who lives only for today. Have you ever heard of a "savings account?" People see you as one who sprinkles joy and fun wherever you go.

OUTER #6: You appear to be the perfect host or hostess who enjoys doting over your guests and loved ones. Others define you as a perfectionist who gets nervous when life doesn't follow what you consider the perfect path. You are reliable and protective, and often sought-after because of your counseling skills.

OUTER #7: You are a good conversationalist; sometimes mystical, sometimes irrational, you always appear to be tuned into more than one reality at a time. Others define you as difficult to get close to but still alluring and unique. There is an air of mystery that surrounds you and makes others want to know who you are and what you are doing with your life. Others define you as mystical and philosophical.

OUTER #8: You appear powerful and influential in the world of business and commerce. You are the executive type, striving to reach the top of your desired ladder. What others think of you is important, as you need respect from your peers. You always seem to be the boss. Solitude is comfortable for you as you can always find some project to work on.

OUTER #9: You appear compassionate and understanding, and your friends seek you out because of this quality. Wise in the ways of the world, you express yourself with an air of having been through it all before. Your sensitivity is apparent and you have no tolerance for injustice.

OUTER #11: You are seen as a transcendental type of person with a set of idealistic goals that you just might reach. Others respect you for your enthusiasm and zest for life. You are a creative personality who inspires others through the example of your life. Through refinement of your creative expression, you will reach social recognition.

OUTER #22: You are seen as the new-age executive. You

have an air of competence that makes your big ideas seem realistic. Your conversation is toward the future. You are seen as someone who wants to help mankind. Your efficiency and diplomacy are a means of making powerful changes that will affect a great number of people. You will achieve success and be recognized for your efforts.

The Destiny Number

The Destiny Number represents a type of power that you must live up to if you are to fulfill your life's purpose. The way to attain this end is through meeting the needs that are represented by the Inner and Outer Personality numbers. If you are not experiencing your Destiny Number on the highest possible level, it is because of failure to integrate the lessons of the Inner and Outer Personality numbers. (Not everyone is living out his or her destiny.)

RULE: Add together all the letters in your full name at birth. This number should be exactly the same as the combined total of your Inner and Outer Personality numbers.

EXAMPLE: DAVID GEORGE POND   5 + 6 = #11 DESTINY

LUCY EVELYN POND   6 + 7 = #4 DESTINY

Now figure out your Destiny Number and learn more about the challenges of destiny that await you.

DESTINY #1: You can best work out your destiny by expressing the unique qualities that separate you from others. A pioneer, you must follow your own calling. Learn to depend on yourself and become a self-made individual. You are a natural leader and should unhesitatingly accept this role. First-hand experience will be the best teacher for you. Watch your tendency to become impatient, which usually results in your becoming arrogant, pushy, or self-righteous. Never settle for second best.

DESTINY #2: Your destiny can best be worked out by cooperating and sharing with others as relationships bring you your greatest joy. Use your gift of diplomacy in bringing divergent groups of people together. Counseling would be an excellent occupation since you are naturally patient and caring with others. Trust your intuition; it won't lead you astray. Your role is that of the nurturer who is working to establish harmony in life.

DESTINY #3: You have the ability to see the bright side in any situation, and some of your mission is connected with just this capacity. Help your friends discover new hope and optimism; you are a natural at this. It is satisfying to see that you have brought new insight to a depressing situation. You are an artist concerned with creative expression, religions of the world, and continually expand your horizons without scattering your precious energy. Wherever you go, you offer people faith and belief in tomorrow; that is your destiny.

DESTINY #4: You can become the cornerstone of life that whole societies are built around. As a worker "par excellence," you can offer practical insights into any project. You have good physical stamina and endurance and will be called upon to organize other people's lives. Your self-discipline and attention to detail will enable you to manifest your goals and inspire others to do the same. You are straightforward, honest, and willing to work for what you get. You are here to serve mankind through the stability you offer. Learn to work within the restrictions you encounter rather than fight them. You are the best-suited of the numbers to carry a heavy work load.

DESTINY #5: You have the potential to become the most friendly number. You would excel in any form of communication or commerce. You like being in the world, and the hardest times for you are when you are stuck with the routines of life with no diversions. You shine in a social atmosphere, meeting new people, and sharing new ideas. You need stimulating contacts, and this is a side of your nature that must not ever be denied. You are here to enjoy the gamut of life's experiences so don't grumble when your life goes through radical changes. You need the challenge. Freedom is of paramount importance to you, so don't fence yourself in. Success comes through your ability to accept the many changes that come your way. Your mission is one of changing, adapting, and living in the moment. You are mobile, and you have the ability to let go of the past faster than anyone else.

DESTINY #6: You are here to create beauty, harmony, and peace in all that you do. Your home life is more important to you than any other aspect of life. You have excellent taste in areas of home decoration or in making any space a comfortable and artistic expression. You prefer peace, but justice comes first; you will fight for what you believe is right. Once you have made a commitment, you will carry through with it. You are most attracted to situations and relationships that need you. You have to feel that there is some purpose to your involvements, or you find it difficult to remain with them. You have natural healing talents and could work with the sick and disadvantaged.

DESTINY #7: This is a life in which there will be many challenges to your value system. You will be forced into situations that will utilize and expand your capacity for discrimination. There will be times when you will have to separate yourself from the mainstream of life to develop your individuality. In time, your accomplishments will be known. Devotion and meditation will bring the answers you seek. You must be willing to endure periods of solitude as you develop your philosophic understanding of life. Your studies will bring you in contact with the occult and the mysterious. Eventually people seek you out to help them unravel the mysteries of life that you have tended to for so long. There is a mystic who dwells deep inside of you.

DESTINY #8: You are here to learn about power, control, and responsibility. You know how to organize groups of people and you will continually be placed in situations that require the use of this skill. You will be at the top of some organization and you will have the test of how to use the power that has been granted you. You want respect from others and you are willing to work for it. You are destined to hold a high position of authority, and you will be called upon to make decisions that affect many people; your judgments will be tested. Happiness comes through gracefully accepting the responsibility and position you are asked to take. In whatever walk of life you choose, you will be successful.

DESTINY #9: This is a lifetime when the test of discrimination surrounds you. You need to believe in some power or source in the universe that is greater than yourself. You need to cultivate a purpose in your life so that others may benefit from your experiences. You will be tested on delusions and deceptions versus belief and faith. Since you are the last of the single digits, you are a composite of all the numbers that have preceded you. You have at your disposal all the gifts and lessons of the other numbers. You must develop forgiveness and compassion for the foibles of being human. You are here to give of yourself and to serve others.

MASTER NUMBERS: Both of the Master Numbers offer more opportunity and more responsibility than the other numbers. With either of these there is a feeling that you have been singled out in this lifetime to perform a special mission. With both of these numbers there is a secret longing to be like everyone else.

DESTINY #11: This number accentuates your intuition and psychic abilities. You are capable of communicating with a broad spectrum of people and you will be called upon to use this skill. Through the life you lead you are offering one of the greatest inspirations; a life with a purpose beyond personal reward. Your visions, and inspiration and ability to see beyond the moment are needed by those you come in contact with. You are a prophet and your message is delivered through your creative expressions. Yours is the task of keeping the dreams and hopes alive in humanity without being crushed by the many rejections of your visions.

DESTINY #22: You are here to lead others and to make some significant changes on this planet. Once you decide on something, you are next to having it. You have a tremendous reserve of personal power at your disposal and you will be tested on the right use of it. Your role is to be a director or a high-level manager, and you must not waste your time on the petty or unimportant. You are a creator and one who manifests your dreams. You will receive recognition for your work.

Predictive Numerology

Predictive numerology works with the areas of your life that are continually changing. Studying this area of numerology is much like studying the transits in astrology. Through knowing the numerical theme that corresponds to these various areas of your life, you can predict how to work most effectively to get the most from the experience. As with the other areas of numerology, the numbers themselves do not cause anything to happen; they simply provide a foundation for understanding the cyclic nature of life. You will work with the same personal numbers that were generated in the chapter on Descriptive Numerology, but in this section you will focus on the cyclic unfolding of the potentials of your birth numbers.

The elements of this section are:
  I.   Your PERSONAL YEAR
  II. Your PERSONAL MONTH
  III. Your PERSONAL DAY

Personal Year

This is the most significant timing indicator used in numerology. This is also the area where there is the most disagreement among numerologists. Some say that the Personal Year begins on your birthday of any given year and others say that it begins on January first of the calendar year. We have come to believe that your Personal Year begins with the change in the calendar year, on January first, and reaches a climax of expression in the month of your birthday.

The procedure for figuring this number is easy and once you have it memorized, you can readily figure the Personal Year of your family and friends. Watch what people are doing in their Personal Years, and see if their actions take on a new meaning through this awareness. Direct observation will be your best teacher.

RULE: Add together the digits of the birthday + birth month + the current year.

EXAMPLE: For someone born on 7/27/1951, the personal year for 1984 is found by adding 7 + 2 + 7 + 1 + 9 + 8 + 4= 38, 3 + 8=11.
The Personal Year is a #11.

Add together the digits of your day, month, and the current year, and discover what this year can mean for you. Take this time to jot down your last nine-year cycle and place a key word next to each of the years. See if this key word corresponds to your Personal Year numbers.

PERSONAL YEAR #1: This is the year of new beginnings and signals a major turning-point in your life. Take your foot off the brake and set something new in motion. If there has been a change that you have been considering, but you have been waiting for the right time, it is here. Take a chance; put yourself out on a limb. This is the year to creatively assert yourself and plunge into new fields of experience. Your intuition will be a better guide to follow than your rational mind. Assert yourself. You are now beginning a cycle that will last for the next nine years, so put your best foot forward and continually remind yourself that the past is over. This is a year to think and plan for the future. Can you creatively assert yourself without stepping on toes? That is the challenge of this year, the whole year from January to December.

PERSONAL YEAR #2: This is a year to slow down, reflect, and substantiate what you started last year. Your personal magnetism is working better for you this year than the aggressive drive that was required last year. You will need to be diplomatic and incorporate tact into all you do. Patience is your key to success. There will be delays in almost all that you do, so know that from the beginning. The key word is cooperation, both in your relationships and in situations as they are presented. Work on establishing peace and harmony and forget about your ego, at least for this year. This is a year when home, family, and security are more important than usual.

PERSONAL YEAR #3: Meet new friends, make new contacts, and broaden your sphere of influence. Be curious. Do whatever possible to improve yourself as a person. This can be a fast-paced, fun, exciting year, but you must watch becoming scattered. Involve yourself in projects of creative self-expression. Friends are more important than usual. Your enthusiastic, "let's go for it" approach to life is interpreted as exciting and inspiring by those around you. Enjoy your social relationships; they form the cornerstone of the year. Don't worry about the details this year, just think big and enjoy yourself. Growth, expansion, and expression are the key words. Ask the question "How far can I push myself?" This is the year to find out.

PERSONAL YEAR #4: This is the year for putting your nose to the grindstone and tending to business. Results come after much effort and long work. Everything you get involved with seems to require more effort than you expect. Keep at it; it will pay off. You must be disciplined this year, as being scattered just won't bring the desired results. Through hard work you will lay a foundation of security that will serve you for many years to come. Be patient; this is the year for work, not play. Pay attention to details and get involved with routines of efficiency. There will be extra responsibility this year, but if you willingly accept, it will not feel like a burden. You can feel yourself confined to a situation that was started three years ago. To bring this project closer to manifestation you will need perseverence and practical application of common sense.

PERSONAL YEAR #5: Socialize and allow yourself some variety of experience. Expect the unexpected, for this is a year when your life will be in a continual state of flux. Your ability to adapt to the ever-changing present will be tested. What you begin this year might not last, as this is a year to experiment, not secure results. You are now half-way through the cycle and feeling a little restless. If people try to pin you down they can find themselves out of your life, as you are experimenting with independence. There is an underlying urge to break up old routines. Be careful of creating difficult and confusing situations out of a need for change.

PERSONAL YEAR #6: Now it is time to once again settle down after a year of uncertainty and change. Formulate your needs concerning personal relationships as a step toward having these needs met. This can be a good year to enjoy the fruits of a relationship. There will be responsibilities to meet and obligations to keep, and the keynote of the year will be service. If you want love and happiness then you must unselfishly give of yourself. Keep in mind all along that the love you get will be equal to the love you give. You are seeking harmony, peace and acceptance and are willing to do whatever is necessary to attain these goals. Unselfishness brings success. Give, give, give and you won't be disappointed this year. Your life will take on a more harmonious note if you listen to advice from family and friends and are willing to make the suggested self-improvements. Some significant conclusions will be reached this year concerning what you value most in life. Being selfish will leave you unrewarded. You are beginning to enjoy your accomplishments.

PERSONAL YEAR #7: This is a year in which you will need time alone to accomplish results. You are searching for more meaning in life. Metaphysical pursuits and occult studies will offer well-needed parts to the rather confusing puzzle. This is a good year for any sort of research and study. You will naturally be more mentally stimulated and it is easier to take time off from social pressures. This is the year for building depth into your personality by searching for meaning and further self-understanding. If your mind is working too hard, causing mental confusion, turn to meditation. Now is the time to utilize any of the spiritually quieting techniques you may know. You will know yourself better by the end of the year and your close friends will probably swear that they don't know you at all. This is a year when you need time away from others to get to know yourself.

PERSONAL YEAR #8: A year for business, finance, and expressing your power potential. Your ambitions are at their peak. Be practical and keep your eyes set on your goals. This is a work year and a time for recognition. Rewards are coming in this time of personal achievement. If you have been resting and sliding on past laurels, this is a time when that, too, gets brought to the public eye. All year long you will be called upon to exercise your ability to organize your life. Pay attention to even the smallest of details and keep your energy output at its most efficient level. If you get behind in your schedule, this can be a time of tremendous mental strain. Try to avoid power struggles. You will get what is due you through hard work and perseverance.

PERSONAL YEAR #9: This year is best used for tying up all the loose ends from previous years' activities and involvements. Something is over in your life and you can feel endings around you all year long. This is not the time to start anything new but rather a time to incorporate lessons from the past. Dreams and fantasies will serve as creative insights for plans that you would be advised to begin in a #1 year. Look at current projects and relationships and ask "What can I do to bring resolution to my current involvement?" Look over the past 9 years and think of them as a cycle that is coming to a close. Be compassionate, loving, and forgiving, especially of yourself. Think of giving to others first; happiness will come through serving others with loving care.

The Master Years will be those special times when there will be more opportunities and more challenges than usual. During these years, you will need to remember that more is being asked of you than at other periods of your life. Try harder during these years and you will experience more fulfillment than you could have dreamed possible.

PERSONAL YEAR #11: Spirituality or religion may play a special role in your life this year. Discussions and sharing with others becomes a priority. Your friends are seeking your advice. Your visions are going to inspire a greater number of people than ever before. Your philosophy can start taking a slant that is for the improvement of humanity. You may be less practical this year but you are certainly more inspired. Share your intuitions with others, as your psychic abilities will be increased. You feel that you have more energy than usual, giving you an I-can-do-it attitude. This is a year to follow your dreams and creative expression, but it is also a year to avoid drugs and alcohol. People will stop listening if your inspired visions turn into fanatic cravings and ravings.

PERSONAL YEAR #22: This is a year to manifest your dreams. The number 22 combines the vision of the number 11 with the practical ability of the number 4. Together, this exemplifies a practical visionary, one who can put dreams into form. Think big this year and don't be afraid to start at the bottom; you will move up quickly. You will be asked to share your ability to organize. You will be working with large groups of people and in some way you will be the leader who knows how to get things done. Don't turn your back on responsibility. Fulfillment comes through sharing with others. Do not waste time on small or petty matters.

Personal Month

Your Personal Month is derived by adding the number corresponding to any given month to the number of your Personal Year.

EXAMPLE: Your birthday is 7/27/1951 and you want to know the Personal Month for January, 1984. First, find the Personal Year for 1984:

$7 + 2 + 7 + 1 + 9 + 8 + 4 + = 38,$
$3 + 8 =$ #11 Personal Year.

Next, add the number of the month to the Personal Year:

$1 + 11 = 12.$

January, 1984 yields a "3" Personal Month for this person.

Remember, these Personal Months operate within the Personal Year, so they give a qualification to the primary meaning of the year.

Personal Day

Your Personal Day is found by adding the number of the day of the month to the number of the Personal Month.

EXAMPLE: The above individual wants to find her Personal Day for January 15, 1984. We already determined that January would be a "3" month for this person, so we add 15 to that to get the Personal Day.

3 + 1 + 5 = 9; January 15, 1984 is a "9" day for her.

One way to see how numerology actually corresponds with your own cycles is to take a calendar and number it with your Personal Months for the year. Next, number each of the days with your Personal Day. This way you will be able to observe the correspondences of the numbers and what they relate to in your personal life. Seeing your own cycles correlated to the rhythms they represent is the most comprehensive way to understand numerology.

Suggested Reading List

Avery, Kevin Quinn. *The Numbers of Life.*
This book contains material on numerological cycles and their effects on the individual. Clearly presented in an occult-free form.

Buess, Lynn M. *Numerology for the New Age.*

Campbell, Florence. *Your Days Are Numbered.*
A clear and simple text with advanced studies for the expert. A widely influential classic, this book explains the method and meaning of numerology.

Goodman, Morris. *Modern Numerology.*

Javane, Faith and Dusty Bunker. *Numerology and the Divine Triangle.*
This work is unique in the correspondences it draws to other systems. We feel that this book can best be utilized by advanced students. Each one of the tarot cards is thoroughly explored along with Bible symbology. This is a fascinating, but rather complex book.

Jordan, Juno. *Numerology, the Romance in Your Name.*
This is an excellent book for all levels of interest, particularly the beginner.

Komaad, Sandor. *Numerology, Key to the Tarot.*
Reveals the secret connection between tarot and numerology with complete instructions to build an "astro-numeric" chart, create a life plan, and interpret card spreads.

Wickenburg, Joanne. *Numerology, a Correspondence Course on Tape.*
This is a thorough and unique way to learn numerology through five 1-hour tapes and a workbook on the subject. We highly recommend this course for the beginner and advanced student.

5

Palmistry

Palmistry is the most accessible of the metaphysical tools; after all, people usually have their hands with them. I used to own a restaurant, and it was my responsibility to hire new people. The birth date of the prospective employee was of some assistance, but palmistry was the most helpful tool for evaluating a person's strengths and weaknesses on the spot. A casual glance at the hand could reveal whether the person would be a good worker or not, and also what type of position in the restaurant would be best for the person's temperament.

The beauty of this for an employer is that much information can be gained by simply watching the person fill out the application form and seeing how they hold their hands during the interview.

...David

Palmistry is the practice of reading the individual character traits and destiny patterns within the hands. Just as no two fingerprints are exactly alike, no two hands are exactly alike. The uniqueness of individuality is recorded in the hands. The advantages of palmistry over other metaphysical systems is twofold. First, it is an actual physical representation of the person's energy field, the lines and shapes being the final physical expression of the more subtle energy being expressed through the individual. Secondly, the availability of palms makes this an extremely mobile tool.

Of all the metaphysical sciences, palmistry is the most easily approached by newcomers. People are more likely to thrust their palms out to be read than they are to ask for a tarot or astrology reading. The personal nature of a palm reading, the holding and touching a person's hand, gives it a warm and friendly appeal. Palmistry is the interpretation of the picture of the individual's life that has been printed on the hands.

If you are a predominantly left-brain person with a keen eye for physical detail, palmistry will come easily for you. To practice palmistry, you will need to develop a discerning eye that can distinguish the most minute differences between hands. The left brain's penchant for practical application of rules will be comfortable with the science of palmistry. There are specific meanings for each of the lines and shapes found within the hand. Synthesizing all of the information found in the hand requires the right brain's ability to draw abstract connections and make generalizations.

If you are a newcomer to the world of metaphysics, plan to devote a few months of study and practice with palmistry's techniques. If you are already involved with other metaphysical systems, especially astrology, palmistry will come more readily. Once you learn the correspondence of the symbols in the hand to symbols in other systems, interpretation will follow naturally.

Modern palmistry could perhaps be more accurately called "handology," as interpretation involves the whole hand and not just the palm. The shape, texture, flexibility, and length of the fingers are just as important as the lines in the palm.

As you refine your awareness of palmistry, you will also refine your interpretations and learn something new from each palm that you observe. You may be inclined to read books on the subject or take a class from a professional palmist, even though this chapter provides a broad base of information that can be easily used. Start to notice how much you can tell about people without their knowledge. This information can allow you to become a better judge of character.

How And Why Does Palmistry Work?

The guiding principle of astrology is the ancient axiom, "As above, so below." In astrology, this concept is disclosed by the birth chart, and in palmistry this knowledge is recorded in the hands. "As above, so below" can also be extended from the microcosm of the hand to the macrocosm of the whole body. The energy of the whole being runs through the hands and records a path by the lines and shapes it leaves. Just as a problem with a car's front-end alignment is indicated by uneven wear of the tires, an imbalance in the individual will be recorded in the hand.

The practice of palmistry has identified the various aspects of the individual character. Palmists know what to expect in a "normal" hand, and when variations appear, they can direct their client's attention to the corresponding area of life. Aside from pinpointing the imbalances, palmistry can also help the individual become aware of talents and character traits that are not being realized.

To begin interpretation, first take a look at the general type of the whole hand, then look at the interaction of the principal parts (thumb and fingers), and finally look to the specific information contained within the lines.

There is no general agreement as to which hand should be read first. We recommend reading your strong hand for the present or actualized self, and the other as the inherent or past self.

The Hand In General

The first step is to divide the hand by visualizing an imaginary line running horizontally across the middle of the palm.

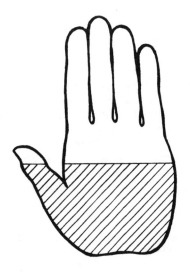

The lower, shaded area of the hand relates to the passive, instinctive part of nature. The upper, non-shaded part of the hand relates to the active side of personal nature and the use of intelligence.

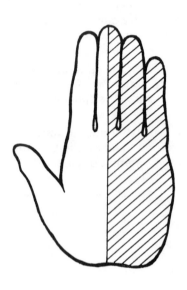

Next, visualize a line running vertically through the hand down the middle of the palm. This division separates the outer (extroverted) and the inner (introverted) parts of the character. The shaded area, which includes half of the middle finger, the ring finger, and the little finger, represents the inner or subjective side of the character which involves feelings and emotions. The unshaded area, including thumb, index finger, and half of the middle finger, represents the exterior side of personality which is involved with goals, ambitions, and the use of the will.

You can also make a general classification about a particular hand by noticing what element it represents. The following descriptions will assist you in making this classification.

THE FIRE HAND: This is an oblong palm with short fingers. The long palm holds the extra reserve of energy for which this hand is known. The short fingers imply impulsive behavior. The owner of this hand has personal flair, can be aggressive, and is certainly a "go-getter" in life. There is a love of adventure and the unpredictable. If you have lost this type of person's attention, you have lost them altogether. They like activity and people, and make better leaders than followers. Highly independent, they like to do what they want to do, when they want to do it.

The Fire palm is often spatulate, wider at one end than the other. The end that is the widest tells where the greatest reserve of energy is, and will give a further clue as to how the Fire element will most typically be expressed.

THE FIRE HAND:

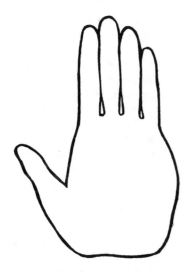

If it is widest at the base of the palm, the physical side of expression will be the most animated. This person is active; in fact, it is difficult for this person to sit still for any length of time. A love of sports and physical or outdoor activities is indicated.

If the palm is spatulate at the top of the palm, the mental side of expression is the most pronounced. This is the visionary who enjoys mental stimulation and challenge. The high mental energy needs to be channeled into creative activities, or there is extreme restlessness.

THE EARTH HAND: This hand has a squarish palm with fingers of approximately the same length as the palm. The palm of the Earth hand should be about as wide as it is long.

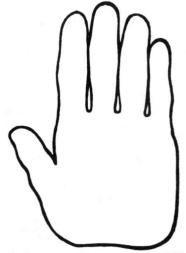

The balance between length of palm and length of fingers reflects a steady, balanced nature. There is the pronounced ability to cope with difficulties. This person is practical, responsible, and resistant to change. As such, he won't give up easily once he has made a stand or commitment. This hand belongs to a worker in life, someone who is down-to-earth and conventional. This person knows how to deal with life just as it is. Patience and loyalty are indicated. Such hands belong to people who are logical and methodical; they seem to simply "sense" what is right for them, and this is the course they follow. Square hands usually have only a few lines.

THE AIR HAND: The palm of the Air hand is longer than it is wide. Its palm is oblong with fingers that are also long and narrow.

This is the hand that is usually singled out as being beautiful and graceful. It belongs to an individual who is impressionable, changeable, and easily influenced by others. This person can be very sociable and is often defined as the life of the party. This person has an eagerness to share new experiences with others, but has no particular love of structure and enjoys trying anything new...at least once. A person with this hand may spread himself too thin with all his varied interests and social connections. This person can be thought of as superficial because he seems to lack emotional depth. The craving for new mental stimulation keeps this person hopping from one situation to another. This person learns quickly and has highly developed mental abilities.

THE WATER HAND: This hand has a short palm in relation to long fingers. There is a roundish look to the whole hand. There is extreme retention of experience indicated. The length of this hand prescribes how long it takes this person to work through experiences. Here we have the sensitive, psychic individual known for strong feelings and a dreamy imagination. This individual makes a better follower than leader and is a person who needs to be needed. This type can be easily overwhelmed by outside experiences. The sensitivity of this hand can be effective with any of the healing arts, or it can be channeled into creative projects such as dance, music, and art. The inner spiritual life is more important to this type than the outer world of reality. A very strong imagination is indicated, which can be a strength in creative endeavors and a weakness in emotional concerns, for there is a tendency to be moody and impressionable.

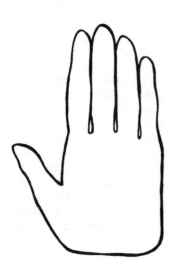

THE MIXED HAND: Just as the name implies, there is going to be a mixture of the qualities of the other four types. No type is going to be an exact fit, but there should be outstanding qualities that place a hand in one category over another. If this does not happen, the hand is MIXED, which will also start to stand out as a category all its own.

This is the hand of versatility and creativity and there is an ability to combine several temperaments.

Other General Characteristics

SMALL HAND: The people with small hands think and act impulsively. Intuitive rather than analytical, they don't use much forethought before acting. Typically, they have good imagination which allows them to think and plan big, but they are not great on the follow-through. This gives them pronounced managerial ability, but they need someone else to carry out their plans.

LARGE HAND: For people with large hands, much thought is put into the plans they make, and they prefer to carry them through themselves. Analytical and excellent with detail, they are good with routines and carry projects through to completion. People with very large hands tend to be moody.

THICKNESS: Does the hand feel either thin or thick? When it is thick and full, it represents physical strength, endurance, and denotes an active nature. There is a good reserve of energy available to this person. If the hand is generally thin, it is representative of a refined and sensitive individual with less physical stamina or strength and more mental energy. This can be the hand of a good conversationalist and a socially active person who does not possess a great deal of physical strength.

FLEXIBILITY: Check the fingers and thumb, and notice how easily they bend and move away from the palm. If they are quite flexible and readily move away from the palm, this quality represents a person who is adaptable to the needs of the moment. But it also tells of one who is easily moved emotionally and might need more internal stability and calmness.

If this is not the case, and you notice stiffness and have difficulty bending the fingers away from the palm toward the back of the wrist, then you are dealing with a person who is rigid, tenacious, and does not make changes well. In this case, all new situations will be examined in light of the past and convention. Security comes first for this type, and there is a great deal of caution. The more stiffness present, the more stubbornness and a greater need for security is indicated.

Now check the thumbs, as they may be different from the fingers. Very flexible thumbs indicate a character that can be easily influenced. Stiff thumbs suggest the inflexible will of strong character; one who is very stubborn and unwilling to try anything new.

COLOR: The general color of the skin is another clue as to the vitality and health of the individual. Relative to a person's race, a hand lacking in color suggests a deficiency of basic vitality. A rosy peach to pink color reflects a healthy physical condition and a similar attitude toward life. A hand that is more red than pink suggests a temperamental person who may be harboring anger. This person can be volatile, but more than likely is just highly active, with lots of "get-up-and-go."

TEXTURE: When the skin is smooth and delicate, it belongs to a person who is impressionable, easily influenced, and generally delicate in nature. A slightly more coarse texture reveals a more hearty system. When the skin is very coarse and rough, you are dealing with a so-called "thick-skinned" individual; one who can be insensitive to his environment and to others.

SPACING: Now, have the person shake all the tension out of their hands and place their elbows on the table with the palms of their hands facing you. What you will be looking for is the general spacing between the fingers, any natural curling toward one of the fingers, or other unusual characteristics that stand out.

The wider the spaces between the fingers, the more openness and need for personal freedom is indicated. If the spaces are naturally wide, fingers spread far apart, it denotes a character that is quite open to new experiences and involvements. This can be a sign of allowing money and emotions to run through life at a careless rate.

When the fingers are more naturally held together, almost touching each other, they signify a conservative type of personality. He or she is not so likely to get involved wtih new situations without a lot of deliberation and evaluation. They tend to be quite cautious and do not easily part with their money, informa-tion, or feelings.

CURLING: When an individual holds up his hands, a portion of the hand or fingers will sometimes curl forward. This occurs when the person is working on something inside himself that is not fully resolved. It can be something he feels insecure about, or perhaps it is signaling an insecure period of life. This curling is a form of shielding and is usually a temporary condition that will last only as long as the problem he is dealing with lasts.

Another method of checking for spacing and curling is to have the person lay his hands, palms down, on a table. The same considerations for spacing apply as when the hands are held in the air. Here, curling is seen slightly differently. Any cupping of the hands, so that the hands do not lay flat on the table, should also be interpreted as curling.

HOLLOW PALMS: Even with the hands lying flat on the table, the center of the palm is depressed rather than flat or bulged. This trait suggests we are dealing with extreme sensitivity and acute perceptiveness. A person with this palm is "thin-skinned," and does not have much protection from outside influences. These individuals are often found working with large groups of people and they definitely have a tendency to give away most of their energy to others.

They need to be reminded to take care of themselves so they will have more reserve to call upon when trying situations occur. They relate well to others because they are willing to invest a great deal into the process of getting to know people.

SPACES BETWEEN THE TWO HANDS: Have the person lay his hands out flat on the table. Are they almost touching each other, or is there a wide space between them?

WIDE SPACE: This represents a type of person ready for action. They are secure enough to experiment with the unknown. This is the eccentric type. There is a tendency for them to jump into situations, scatter their energy, and then not complete what they started.

NARROW SPACE: These people tend to be content with the way things are. Their primary need is for security rather than adventure. They will exhibit caution and think before they act.

MODERATE SPACE: This represents the person who excer-cises temperance with indulgences and new experiences. He is not afraid to enter new experiences, as long as it is tempered with a degree of common sense.

HANDS TOUCHING EACH OTHER: The person is going through a very inhibited time of life. He is coping with all he can, and does not want to take on anything new.

JUST THE THUMBS TOUCHING: An unusual degree of tact, diplomacy, and consideration is evident. These are the perfectionists who require order in their lives.

FINGER LENGTH: In judging finger length, it is important to remember that you are judging the length in respect to the rest of the hand the finger is attached to. It is a relative process and requires you to look at the whole hand before you make a judgment. Fingers are considered long if the middle finger is as long as, or longer than, the palm. They are considered short if the middle finger is less than approximately 7/8 of the length of the palm (use a ruler).

Long-fingered people have a penchant for intellectual activity. Thinking, talking, writing, and the entire communication process will be emphasized in their natures. There is a tendency to be short-sighted and to miss the overall picture, yet they are good thinkers on abstract levels.

Short-fingered people are better at sensing the overall picture and make excellent managers and organizers. They are not as facile at seeing all the details, but they can get help from their long-fingered friends. These fingers belong to those who are motivated by gut-level responses. Action, rather than thinking and planning, is their keynote to success.

FINGER SHAPE: The shape of the ends of the fingers also give clues to individual characteristics. There are basically four types of fingers:

THE SQUARE FINGER: Reflects a practical, hard-working nature. This is the down-to earth type that can handle routine, structure, and organization. They have balanced thoughts, are decisive, and have a good sense of responsibility.

THE ROUND FINGER:
This belongs to the imaginative, easy-going type of individual. These people are sensitive to the needs of others, are adaptable, and have reliable intuition. They also have an inherent appreciation of the arts.

THE POINTED FINGER:
This is the finger of the psychic, idealistic type of person. They are sensitive and cannot always rationally deal with all the information they pick up psychically. They are extremely restless and changeable, and have a tendency to be overwhelmed easily.

THE SPATULATE FINGER: This represents an energetic, original, and inventive type of person. They not only can generate dreams, but can also follow them through to actualization. Seeking adventure, they tend to be quite impulsive.

THE PHALANGES OF THE FINGERS: The fingers have three natural sections or phalanges. Each phalange relates to a different type of behavior. The phalange that is the longest in a hand shows where the dominant focus in life will be.

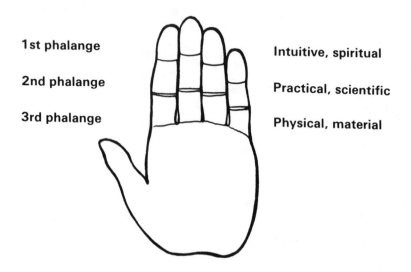

1st phalange	**Intuitive, spiritual**
2nd phalange	**Practical, scientific**
3rd phalange	**Physical, material**

Here is where you can start to use your own skills of interpretation. Notice which section of the finger is the longest to discover where there will be a major focus of energy and expression.

FIRST PHALANGE: The major focus in life is artistic, musical, or spiritual.

SECOND PHALANGE: The major focus will be of a scientific or practical application of energy. This is the type of person who likes to make plans and then follow them through to completion.

THIRD PHALANGE: The major focus will be physical or sensual. Material and emotional concerns will be highlighted.

At this time, you should notice whether the fingers are smooth or knotty.

SMOOTH FINGERS: There is a lack of knots or knuckling, and they are representative of versatile, adaptable, and intuitive people. There is a lack of tenacity on projects as these people are often sensitive and moody.

SHORT: These are the people who will jump into a project or a relationship without a real understanding of the details required to actually pull everything together. They focus on the broad, general picture.

LONG: These persons like to know what they are getting themselves into before they jump. They have a tendency to vacillate while considering all the options.

KNOTTY FINGERS: Action becomes deliberate and thoughtful with these people. The more knotty the fingers, the longer it will take them to make up their minds. An industrious and orderly approach to life is indicated.

FIRST KNOTS (those closest to the fingertips): These are called "philosophic knots." They usually denote an orderly, detailed type of thinking. Before people with first knots accept an idea, they will have to prove it to themselves.

SECOND KNOTS: For these people, action is methodical, and they have good self-discipline. This is not the sign of an abstract thinker, but certainly is of one who actualizes plans.

BOTH ARE KNOTTED: Precise and logical individuals are indicated. A strong need to control their world can make this type appear cold and calculating. Very fixed thinking patterns make it very difficult for them to change their minds once they are made up.

The Individual Fingers

Each finger represents a different aspect of the total individual. Each of the fingers is given a planetary name, and its meaning corresponds directly to that planet in astrology. Interpretation comes when you look at each finger separately and know the meaning of the finger and its distinguishing characteristics, such as smooth, knotty, spatulate, round, etc.

INDEX FINGER: Ruled by Jupiter. This finger relates to confidence, leadership ability, and desire for growth past existing boundaries. Religious leadership and ambition are also shown by this finger. This is the finger of self-confidence. Executive ability, along with the power to exert influence on others, is shown by this finger.

MIDDLE FINGER: Ruled by Saturn. Here is where we accept or reject responsibility. Moral and ethical qualities are shown by this finger. Truth-searching, introspection, and inner strength are the qualities represented. The ability to balance inner and outer responsibilities with a sense of duty and self-control is shown here. Discernment and judgment are also revealed here as are the needs for perfection.

RING FINGER: Ruled by Apollo. (Apollo was the Greek god who was the patron of the arts.) Self-expression, creativity, and interest in the arts are represented by this finger. It shows one's ability to feel contentment and satisfaction with life. The willingness and ability to be in tune with the inner self, the total creative self, is manifested here.

LITTLE FINGER: Ruled by Mercury. Denotes a willingness to relate to others and represents all verbal communication. The little finger shows the person's capacity for brilliance, eloquence, and commerce. Money-making abilities by the use of the mind are exposed here.

FINGERPRINT PATTERNS: It is well known that no two fingerprints are exactly alike. Fingerprints can be used to identify an individual with no other information available. Although unique, all fingerprints fall within three major categories. By far the most common pattern is the Loop. The Arch and the Whorl are the other two possible categories.

THE LOOP: This is the pattern found in the vast majority of hands. If the fingertips can be considered the receptors of energy, then the prints are the patterns in which the energy is received. With the Loop, the energy is received from two directions; from the spiritual and from the physical. This integration creates a balance.

THE WHORL: The whorl is a circular pattern that is not very common. This is a free-wheeling type of energy field that is not bound by the elemental forces and represents a highly creative person who can be inventive in any situation. They want to do things their own way, without following the norm.

THE ARCH: This pattern, also uncommon, is considered the most physical. This can represent two types of individuals. The first type tends to be immersed in materiality to the point of indulgence. The second type can be in tune with nature-spirits and have an intuitive sense of rhythms and cycles.

All fingerprint patterns can be categorized into one of these three groupings. It is possible for all three patterns to be found on a single hand. Because of this, you will want to interpret the type of print for the individual finger on which it is found. All irregularities should be considered for interpretation. For example, if all but one of the fingerprints are loops, and one is a whorl pattern, the finger the whorl is on will stand out as special. This finger, and the area of life it represents, will be where this individual will be fulfilling himself creatively.

You can even check the mounts and the palm to see if there are any distinctive patterns to be found. It sometimes happens that a whorl will be found on a particular mount. This represents an area of special creative potential.

The Thumb

Among the fingers, the thumb is unique. Being opposed to the fingers, it allows the fingers to grasp or to fulfill their potential.

In palmistry, the thumb shows the person's ability to apply will, logic, and vital energy in fulfilling goals. It represents personal will power.

1st phalange:
Expression of will

2nd phalange:
Reasoning and logic

3rd phalange:
Vital energy and passion

1ST PHALANGE OF THE WILL: Here we have an indicator of how an individual uses his will. The principal clues will be thickness and rigidity. A thick thumb indicates an individual with a forceful will. If it is also rigid, then you have someone who will get what he or she wants regardless of the cost. A less fleshy phalange implies a more yielding nature. The strength of this type is in their ability to adapt. The weakness is in their inability to stay with a project to completion. Ideally, the first phalange should be somewhat shorter than the middle phalange. If longer, there can be an excessive use of will power.

2ND PHALANGE OF LOGIC: This represents the ability to consider the situations of life in a logical, rational manner. A thick phalange suggests an individual who has set opinions and is not open to reason. These people know what they know and that is that. A thin second section conveys openness and an ability to consider all sides of a question. There is great diplomacy and tact in expression. The drawback of this type is their vacillation in making decisions. This is the opposite of the person with a thick phalange who makes quick and consistent decisions. Once you know what position a person with a thick second phalange will take on an issue, you can depend on him to not change his mind.

3RD PHALANGE OF VITAL ENERGY: This phalange, traditionally known as the MOUNT OF VENUS, appears to be the root of the thumb. Its function is that of a reservoir of the physical energy available for the rest of the thumb to use. The firmer and higher the Mount, the greater the physical energy. The Mount actually shows how much physical energy the person has, so the larger it is, the more energy he or she has.

With a well-developed third phalange, you can expect an outgoing, active person. They are usually involved in some daily form of physical exercise: dance, a movement class, or sports. In whatever they do, they carry themselves with physical grace. They have a high appreciation of beauty, friendship, luxury, and indulgences. Family and homelife are of a primary concern.

When this phalange is thin or underdeveloped, the potential for liveliness and "letting go" has to be cultivated in the person. This person needs more physical exercise, and needs to get out and start being more carefree. They tend to be self-contained and detached from the world. Their low vitality keeps them from a full participation in life.

OTHER THUMB CHARACTERISTICS:

SHORT THUMB: A thumb is considered short if it ends near the base of the index finger. This shows the person has difficulty in directing will.

LONG THUMB: If the thumb extends beyond the middle joint of the index finger, it is considered long. This is the sign of the high-achiever; ambitious and assertive in his approach to life.

The longer the thumb, the more forceful the expression of the personality.

WAISTED THUMB: When the thumb has a waist (narrowing) at the second phalange, the person is said to be a diplomat with great tact. This person can easily adapt to or get himself out of any difficulty.

The angle at which the thumb is usually held away from the hand gives clues as to how the person approaches life.

CLOSE (0° to 30°): A lack of independence and confidence is shown. They can be very tight with their money and emotions.

WIDE (30° to 60°): This is the generous type of person that likes sharing, cooperating, and giving to others. This person is quite independent in his approach to life.

VERY WIDE (60° to 90°): These people tend to be anti-social with a strong, driving need to always have their own way. They need to beware of selfish motivations.

The Fingers In Relation To Each Other

Each finger represents a different aspect of the total individual, but how are each of these parts operating in terms of the total? This is found by looking at the whole hand and noticing the finger lengths in relation to each other. Also note any special leaning of one finger toward another.

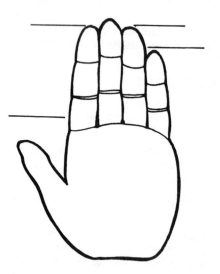

AVERAGE LENGTH OF FINGERS: The middle finger is normally the longest finger, with the ring and index fingers being equal in length to each other. They should measure midway up the first phalange of the Saturn finger. The little finger, Mercury, should measure half-way up the first phalange of the Apollo finger. The thumb, when held up to the index finger, is considered to be of average length if it reaches to the midpoint of the third phalange of the index finger.

Much information can be gained about the individual character of a person by noting any peculiarities in the finger lengths. If a finger is longer than expected, it is said to intensify its characteristics within the individual. There is a greater potential expression of the energy represented by that finger. There is also the danger of becoming dependent on the function of that particular finger to the neglect of the others.

If a finger is shorter than you would expect, an underexpression of the energy it represents should be suspected. This is particularly important if this shows up in the thumb. This indicates that the will power to maintain a sustained effort is lacking, and the individual will have to reinforce this deficiency with some other character strength in order to achieve his goals.

BENDING AND LEANING OF THE FINGERS: Ideally, the fingers should be straight in order to receive and express the energy the fingers represent. Straight fingers represent clear perception. It sometimes happens that one or more of the fingers leans, or is bent, toward another. When this is the case, the bent finger is being influenced by the one it is leaning toward. This creates a bias in perception; a slanted view in relation to the meaning of the finger in question.

As example: all the fingers of the hand bend toward the Saturn finger. This represents an urge to establish order, discipline, and structure. Another example: the entire hand bends away from the thumb. This represents an inward searching in life; the pull for social involvement is minimal.

THE MOUNTS: Studying the mounts has a twofold purpose. It serves as a map of the palm, with reference points for your observation, and the actual condition of the mounts gives you clues to the total makeup of the character they represent.

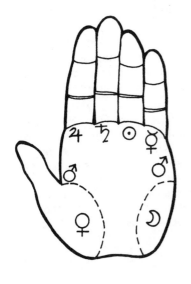

☉	Sun
☽	Moon
☿	Mercury
♀	Venus
♂	Mars
♃	Jupiter
♄	Saturn

The mounts are the fleshy pads that appear in the areas shown on the chart. They are storehouses of energy for the fingers, thumb, heel of the hand, and the inner and outer sides of the hand. These reservoirs are given planetary names, and the energy they store is related to the corresponding planet.

The finger mounts are the elevated pads at the top of the palm, just beneath the fingers. They are given the same name as the finger to which they are attached. The finger is seen as the expression of the planetary energy, and the mount is seen as the capacity for that expression. Things to watch for are the strength and size of the mount, as well as its location. Experience will tell you what is a strong mount and what is not. Generally, a mount is considered strong if it is elevated and firm to the touch. This is a sign of vitality and an adequate energy reservoir for the finger to draw on. If the mount is flat or flabby, it is considered weak, and the energy connected with it would be less than desirable for the person's needs.

JUPITER MOUNT: Located directly under the index finger. If this mount is strong, firm, and directly under the finger, the person is said to have abundant energy available to satisfy his or her ambitions. Jupiter rules a person's desire to expand all spheres of influence and receive rewards from society. The mount has much to do with the confidence a person will have in these endeavors. A strong mount indicates plenty of confidence. A weak mount shows a corresponding lack of poise and self-assurance.

If the mount is located to the side of center, so that it is between the Jupiter and Saturn fingers, then the ambition for success will be more cautious and conservative. The person will more likely be linked to groups and organizations rather than to individual success.

SATURN MOUNT: The mount at the base of the Saturn finger indicates a person's ability to adhere to discipline. A strong mount here shows a person with a rather serious, cautious nature, with a life of duty and responsibility. This person naturally gravitates to positions of authority and hard work. An over-developed mount belongs to a person with a morose and gloomy disposition, one who sees the dark cloud in front of every silver lining. The life of this person is usually filled with restraints.

When the mount is underdeveloped, or absent, the person is

less likely to be found in restrictive positions. This person is less constrained in life than the individual with the developed Saturn mount.

MOUNT OF APOLLO: This mount deals with creativity, social ability, and appreciation of beauty. The qualities of Venus are akin to this mount. A strong Apollo mount reveals a strong creative identity and delicacy in dealing with other people.

The strength of this mount is also a social-involvement indicator. The stronger the mount, the more gregarious and outgoing the personality, and the more likely the person is to be involved with the arts.

A weak mount here indicates shyness and a sense of inadequacy. If the mount is shifted toward Saturn, the creative identity is more serious, and the person is likely to feel a need for a great deal of discipline in order to be productive. If the mount is shifted toward Mercury, the urge is to express creativity through communication or business ventures. When this mount is flat or weak, the person has difficulty maintaining creative inspiration.

THE MERCURY MOUNT: The mount of Mercury is an indicator of how a person feels about their communication abilities and the practical concerns of everyday living. When the mount is strong and highly developed, it represents confidence in these matters. This is also indicative of a practical mind with good business sense.

When the mount is low or underdeveloped, there is a corresponding impracticality in business and money concerns. This person can also be inarticulate. The strength of concentration is low and needs to be built up when this mount is flat.

Vertical lines on this mount show healing abilities.

THE MOUNT OF THE MOON: Located at the heel of the hand, opposite the thumb. Creativity and imagination are shown in this area.

A well-developed Moon mount denotes one of great imagination, perhaps a creative writer. If the mount is fleshy all the way up to the little finger, psychic abilities are indicated.

If the mount is weak or pale, you can expect an underdeveloped imagination. The sensitive, feeling aspect of life may not be trusted by a person with this type of mount.

THE MOUNT OF VENUS: Located at the base of the thumb,

the mount of Venus deals with physical love, pleasure, vitality, and indulgences. The firmer and higher the mount, the greater the amount of physical energy available. (See 3rd phalange of the thumb for other interpretations.)

THE MOUNT OF MARS: There are two of these mounts found on either side of the palm. They both deal with courage and assertiveness. The mount that is closest to the thumb deals with active aggression and the general life force. Overdevelopment denotes a hostile, quarrelsome personality. If underdeveloped, it shows a lack of ability to defend one's self and to say "no."

The outer mount, opposite the thumb and over the Moon mount, rules self-control. If it is well-developed, a balanced, mature individual is indicated. If soft, it represents one who does not have much self-control.

The Lines

By this time it should be evident that studying the hands is much more than the name PALMISTRY implies. It is only now, after all the characteristics of the hand as a whole have been observed, that we actually look at the palms themselves. There are two major categories of lines. The major lines include the life line, the heart line, the head line, and the fate line. The minor lines will be studied separately, and they include the Apollo line, the Mercury line, the girdle of Venus, the relationship lines, and the travel lines.

THE MAJOR LINES

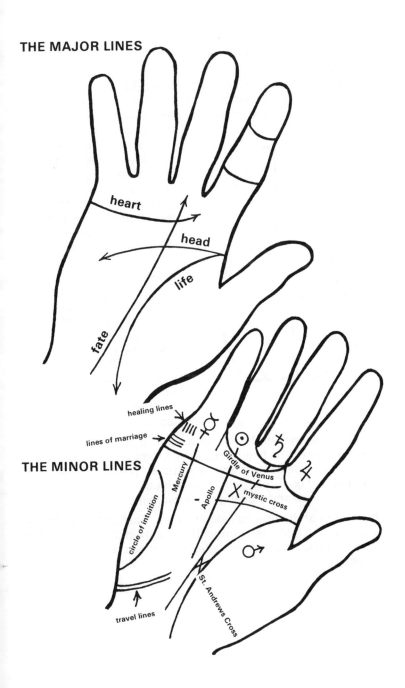

heart

head

life

fate

THE MINOR LINES

healing lines

lines of marriage

Mercury

circle of intuition

Apollo

Girdle of Venus

mystic cross

St. Andrews Cross

travel lines

The Major Lines

THE LIFE LINE: The life line, which starts between the thumb and the index finger and embraces the Venus mount, is the main clue to a person's vitality, health, and personality. The sweep of

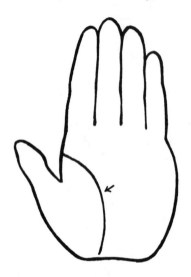

the arc that it makes refers to how outgoing the personality is. The wider the arc, the more outgoing the personality. If there are any changes in the degree of the arc, this represents a change in the direction of the personality. If the arc starts off narrow and changes to a wider arc, that represents a person who starts life rather shy and retiring and then develops a more outgoing personality. The reverse is also true. If the arc starts off wide and becomes more narrow, the personality changes to a more inward focus.

The origin of the life line is important. It will normally start midway between the beginning of the thumb and the beginning of the index finger. The higher it starts on the hand, the more ambitious and goal-oriented the individual. The lower it starts, the more inward and yielding the personality.

The quality of the line has significance. Basically, the deeper and clearer the line, the stronger the vitality of the person. If the line is chained, broken, or fades out, these are all clues to diminished vitality.

TIMING ON THE LIFE LINE: The life line gives the best clues on the hand for the timing of events and situations. However, even at best, it is still only an estimate of approximate time.

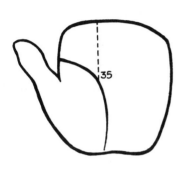

To measure time in the hand, visualize a line running down the middle of the Saturn finger. Where this line intersects the life line marks the half-way point of life; approximately 35 years of age. Divide the two halves of the line into thirds, fifths, or sevenths to define smaller increments of time. Other students of palmistry have used the degrees of arc to measure time. You will have to experiment to discover which system works for you.

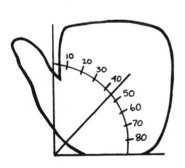

Traumas, accidents, and periods of ill health are indicated by breaks, crosses, and other disruptions in the life line. You can use the approximate timing method to see whether the event has already happened or if it is in the future. If it is in the future, you may want to examine the person's lifestyle to see if they are setting themselves up for an accident.

THE HEAD LINE: The head line shows the quality of intelligence a person possesses. (It does not designate the quantity, but rather the type.) The straighter the head line, the more logical

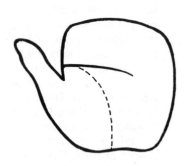

and practical the person. The more the line dips toward the lunar mount, the more a person draws on intuition. As in all lines, the deeper and clearer the line, the stronger the energy represented by the line. If the line is broken, fragmented, or chained, the person's ability to maintain mental concentration is decreased.

The placement of the beginning of the head line in relation to the life line shows how the mental faculties are integrated into the whole of the person's life. There are four possible points of origin of the line:

JUST TOUCHING THE LIFE LINE: This is the normal beginning of the line. Denotes a harmonious interblending of mental functions with the action of life.

ABOVE THE LIFE LINE: This represents the highly individualistic thinker. This person is likely to be abstract and lofty. The wider the gap between the two lines, the more individualistic the mind. An extremely wide gap belongs to the person whose thoughts are not at all conditioned by others.

BELOW THE LIFE LINE: These persons cannot separate thoughts from feelings. Their thinking is impulsive and they have a tendency to jump to conclusions. This type can be argumentative, fiesty, and when you challenge their thinking you are challenging their basic integrity, which can make them even more defensive.

MERGED WITH THE LIFE LINE: This shows the type of person who is strongly conditioned by their parents, environment, and early education. The longer the marriage of the two lines, the longer the person's thinking was conditioned by others. Where the head line separates from the life line is where the person starts being more independent in thinking.

Branches on the head line show adaptability and variety of mental interests. If there is a tassel on the end of the head line, it represents mental energy that is easily overloaded. This is a clue that the individual had difficulty in focusing on specific problems.

THE HEART LINE: The heart line, as the name implies, governs the responses of your heart. The ability to express emotions and affection are shown by the quality of this line.

The heart line is more varied than the two previously discussed lines. It typically starts underneath the Mercury finger, and it usually ends under the Jupiter mount. If the line is clear, with no

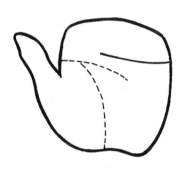

breaks, and gently slopes toward the Jupiter mount, it is considered normal, and the individual will be able to express his love easily and stay committed with the heart. If the line is faint or non-existent, the person's emotions are ruled by the head, and it is not easy for him to express affection. When the line is broken, it could indicate emotional disappointments and painful separations.

When the line branches, it shows that the heart is easily captured and that it is harder to stick to one love. This is the sign of the flirt. When the heart line dips down at the end, there is an inward turning of the affection. This person is not open or demonstrative in his love life. In a male hand, this is said to represent a certain amount of femininity; in a female hand with this characteristic, masculine qualities are strengthened.

The length of this line is also a clue to the person's love life. A long line is one that extends all the way to the Jupiter mount, and this represents someone who is extremely confident, although rather reckless, in dealings of the heart. A medium line extends to a point midway between the Jupiter and Saturn mounts. This indicates a conservative, thoughtful approach to love. Neither overpossessive, nor exhibiting a need for excessive freedom, this person often has long-lasting, compatible relationships. When the line is short, it stops under the mount of

Saturn, and the conservative, cautious, serious nature of Saturn influences the expression of the heart. This person can be very possessive and suspicious in love. It is as if he doesn't see himself as worthy of receiving love, and he is always suspicious of the motives of those who love him.

When there is a line or lines between the head and heart line, it indicates a person who is overly-analytical of feelings. He may have experienced disappointments which have made him cautious in his approach to love.

THE FATE LINE: The fate line typically starts at the base of the palm, and runs vertically through the palm toward the Saturn finger. The length and quality of this line, as well as where it begins, tells of the person's ambitions and independence.

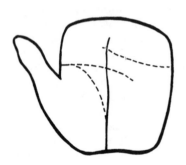

Generally, the stronger the line, the more control a person has of his or her destiny. If the line starts low in the hand, near the wrist, it reveals a person who has been ambitious all through life. If the line starts higher up on the hand, it indicates a person who won't really get ambitious until later in life.

If the line starts in the middle of the hand, it represents an independent person. This type creates his own opportunities in life.

If the origin of the line is inside the life line, it describes someone with ambitions that are strongly conditioned by his family. He often depends upon and receives family assistance in reaching his goals. When the line begins on the Lunar mount, it represents a person whose destiny is going to be affected by influence. He often chooses a career that puts him in the public eye.

When the line ends at the head line, it represents an ambition that quiets down after the person reaches the age of thirty. This person usually finds what he wants to do early in life, and he stays with it. When the line continues past the head line and ends at the Saturn mount, the individual is more likely to be ambitious throughout life.

Sometimes it happens that the line breaks and starts again, or it changes direction. This always indicates a change in career or direction of ambition. This line can also be missing on some hands. Generally, this indicates a "will-o'-the-wisp" type of personality. These people are less inclined to be at the mercy of their fates. They have the opportunity to choose their direction and to create situations of luck for themselves.

The Minor Lines

The minor lines are found less frequently than the major lines. The very presence of any of these lines indicates that the corresponding energy is available to the individual. As in the study of all lines, the depth and quality of the line indicates what degree of influence the line has.

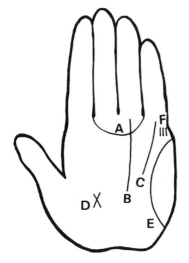

A — *The Girdle of Venus*

B —— *The Apollo Line*

C — *The Mercury Line*

D — *St. Andrew's Cross*

E —— *Circle of Intuition*

F —— *Healing Lines on Mercury*

THE GIRDLE OF VENUS: The Girdle of Venus is the half-circle ring that starts under the Apollo finger, encircles the mount of Saturn, and ends between the Jupiter and Saturn fingers. This is a sign of the love of sensation. These are very sensual people. In the positive expression, they are people who are very affectionate and have refined sensitivities; they appreciate good food, music, and art. Negative expressions of this aspect are found in escapism through drugs and alcohol. These people also have a tendency to indulge in food and sex to excess.

LINE OF APOLLO: This is the vertical line that runs under the ring finger. This is always an indicator of the potential for creative expression. The Apollo finger is seen as the finger of aesthetics and creative self-expression, and when there is a line beneath this finger, these areas of life are extremely important to this individual. Sometimes there is more than one line here, and this is an indicator of more than one creative interest. If the line is branched, it is a sign that the creative energy is likely to scattered and ineffectual.

THE MERCURY LINE: This line is easy to identify if present, as it is the only diagonal line running from the life line toward the mount of Mercury. This line signifies great depth of perception. These people are able to understand the forces that are lying just beneath the surface. Because of this perception, they appear to have strong intuition, although it is more accurate to say that their logical facility has greater range than that of most people. A heightened ability to communicate information which appears hidden to others makes these people good writers, counselors, and psychics.

ST. ANDREW'S CROSS: This marking, found near the base of the palm, between the life line and the fate line, is said to give life-saving abilities. This can mean literally plucking someone out of a river, yet it can also be the case where this person has the ability to save others from a destructive way of life and put them back on a healthy track.

CIRCLE OF INTUITION: This marking, found on the Lunar mount, is actually quite rare. Whenever it is found, the person can draw on a high degree of intuition. A more common form of this line is the "angle of intuition." which is found in the same place but is formed by two straight lines rather than a semicircle. When this is the case, intuition is there but it is not quite as free-flowing or psychic.

HEALING LINES: These are the three or four short vertical lines that occasionally appear on the mount of Mercury. Those with healing lines are said to have healing ability and they can sense what an ailing person needs in order to recover. Also, their touch is very healing in itself.

Conclusion

If you want to further your studies of palmistry in even greater detail, here is a list of books to assist you in your studies.

Suggested Reading

Anderson, Mary. *Palmistry.* Samuel Weiser, New York, NY, 1980.

Brenner, Elizabeth. *Hand in Hand.* Celestial Arts. Millbrae, CA, 1981.

Gettings, Paul. *The Book of the Hand.* Paul Hamlyn, London, 1965.

Hipskind, Judith. *Palmistry, the Whole View.* Llewellyn Publications, St. Paul, MN, 1977.

West, Peter. *Life Lines, An Introduction to Palmistry.* The Aquarian Press, Wellingborough, Northamptonshire, 1981.

Wilson Joyce. *The Complete Book of Palmistry.* Bantam Books, 1971.

6

Applied Metaphysics

The application of metaphysics goes beyond divination; it becomes a way of life with a broad range of use. The study of metaphysics affords the opportunity to organize the aspects of our lives that go beyond what is physically apparent. In this section, we will present a variety of these techniques for viewing the various parts of your character.

The senses are able to receive and interpret within a certain range of frequencies. A television set is sensitive to one range of vibration, and a radio is sensitive to yet another. Reality is not limited to what television, radio, or your five senses can perceive. In other words, the limits of your physical senses do not necessarily define the limits of all reality. Each device is sensitive to a specific, but limited, range of frequency.

Your "self" as you know it is made up of other parts that are just as real as the physical body, but which are not visible to the senses. These other parts are known as energy fields, auras, and chakras. Understanding these aspects of yourself can be helpful in giving you a more encompassing view of life. To understand them, it is necessary to go beyond logical thinking to allow the abstract, intuitive part of your mind to help.

The journey into higher consciousness requires you to learn to fully operate the exquisite mechanism that we call "the body." This involves becoming familiar with a subtle realm of perception, but the effects and implications are a part of your everyday world, and are not as subtle as you might think. Through awareness of these centers, you will enhance your holistic expression of self and experience more energy and balance in life.

Chakras

The different energy fields connected to the body are much like various frequencies through which human life can be expressed.

These energy centers are called *chakras,* from the Hindu word for wheel. The chakras are thought to be spinning wheels, creating a vortex of energy. The energy spins more slowly at the base of the spine, becoming faster and brighter as it reaches the top of the spine. Breath, consciousness, and awareness are the tools that are required to keep the energy spinning.

The chakras create the energy field that is known as the luminous body or aura, which surrounds all forms of life. There are some sensitive people who perceive the aura as colors or an electrical field, but a great number do not perceive it at all. The aura is constantly changing and is a manifestation of the energy of your entire being. How you physically, emotionally, mentally, and spiritually feel is reflected in the aura. It is to your direct advantage to be sensitive to this energy field in yourself and in those with whom you come in contact.

The chakras are the batteries for the body. They receive and store energy by interacting with the universal life force. They then direct the energy to supply the needs of the body. The freedom with which energy can flow back and forth between you and the universe is in direct correlation to the total health and well-being you may experience.

Any blocks or restrictions that you might have in either reception or expression of this life energy will result in a malfunction of the organism as a whole and will be experienced as disease, discomfort, lack of energy, or an ailment. By acquainting yourself with your chakras, how they work, and how they should operate when totally healthy, you can diagnose your own blocks and restrictions and have some guidelines for relieving them. (By "blocks" we mean restrictions -- complete blockage would result in disconnection with the universal life force, or death.) Everyone has chakras and all of them are functioning. The degree of efficiency is the factor that varies between individuals and between different stages in your life. The chakras can more simply be viewed as seven pathways to consciousness, which work together to create a sense of joy and holistic love for life.

The chakras are associated with the endocrine gland system. Their placement in the body corresponds with the location of these ductless glands, and the meaning of each individual chakra is closely connected to the function of the corresponding gland. The chakras are located along the spine and positioned just in front of it.

NO.	CHAKRA	GLAND	ELEMENT	FUNCTION	COLOR
1	Root	Gonads/ovaries	Earth	Security	Red
2	Sacral	Spleen	Water	Sensation	Orange
3	Solar	Adrenals	Fire	Power	Yellow
4	Heart	Thymus	Air	Harmony	Green
5	Throat	Thyroid	Ether	Creativity	Sky Blue
6	Third Eye	Pituitary	Thought	Telepathy	Indigo
7	Crown	Pineal	Spirit	Wisdom	Violet

Areas Of Consciousness

PHYSICAL: Root and Sacral chakras
EMOTIONAL: Solar Plexus and Heart chakras
MENTAL: Solar Plexus, Heart, Throat, Third Eye, and Crown chakras
PSYCHIC: All chakras
SPIRITUAL: All chakras

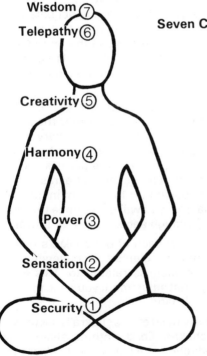

Wisdom ⑦
Telepathy ⑥
Creativity ⑤
Harmony ④
Power ③
Sensation ②
Security ①

Seven Centers Of Consciousness

Within The Body

You will experience more sustained energy and interact with more people as you move toward the higher centers.

Real happiness only be comes possible as the ego subsides and you spend more time in the Heart chakra.

You will interact with fewer people and experience less sustained energy as you allow yourself to be preoccupied with the lower centers of consciousness.

The chakras are both receptive and expressive of the universal life energy. The receptive mode is spontaneous as the energy is received through the Crown chakra and distributed to the other chakras. The expression of energy is the second half of the cycle, where considered responses are based on learning from experience. The expressive part of the cycle requires consciousness and awareness.

"Kundalini" is a term from Eastern philosophy that is helpful in understanding this process. Basically, Kundalini means serpent power. In this understanding, the Kundalini is said to be coiled at the base of the spine. Through different situations, exercises, and meditations the Kundalini is said to uncoil and move up the series of chakras, releasing the energy stored in each chakra that it contacts. Of course, there is not a serpent in the spine, but this method of visualization offers an image that helps us understand the process.

To raise the Kundalini to its highest potential, it is necessary to balance the expression of it at each successive chakra, starting at the Root chakra. If the energy of the chakra is not balanced, the needs represented by the chakra will demand attention to the point that it would make it difficult to use the energy in a personally creative way. When the needs of a chakra become balanced, the Kundalini energy naturally and spontaneously rises to the next highest energy center.

The lower three chakras represent biological, physical life. The energy of these first three chakras is used to animate the physical requirements of our being. Each chakra has primary needs associated with it. When the needs are met in a way that is harmonious with the environment, balance results. It is helpful, though, to be aware of the fact that these three chakras are, by nature, insatiable. If you are looking for fulfillment in life only through these first three chakras, you will experience the frustration of never quite having enough security, sex, or power.

The following is a description of each of the chakra's needs. Use it as a guide. When you have problems and challenges, ask yourself which chakra the problem is related to. This is an effective method of knowing what adjustment you need to make to move beyond the problem at hand.

FIRST CHAKRA: The primary need of this chakra is security. It is the most instinctive of all chakras. Food, clothing, shelter, and protection, as well as reproduction at a biological level, are the necessities to which it responds. SURVIVAL is the basic need.

SECOND CHAKRA: The primary needs of this center are sensual and sexual gratification. Feeling attractive and able to draw things toward you is another need of the second chakra, as is the desire to lose yourself in the world of sensation.

THIRD CHAKRA: To be self-assertive and to have a sense of your own power is the drive connected with this chakra. Ability to recognize yourself as an individual, and being capable of defending yourself and saying "no" are also requirements of the Solar chakra. Power, courage, and manipulation are all aspects of this center.

In the first three centers, you do not experience unconditional love. This will only occur as you move into the fourth center. The filters through which you see life at the first three centers force you to deal with people as objects that are either getting in the way of your needs, or facilitating the process of having your needs met.

FOURTH CHAKRA: A connection transcending the differences between self and others must be felt. The fourth chakra is the center that joins the individual with the collective. The lower three chakras deal with the individual; separate and against the universal. The upper three chakras are the collective aspects of the self. The Heart chakra is where the upper and lower aspects of self meet and merge. From this point, you see yourself reflected in everyone you meet. There is a feeling of unconditional love and acceptance for all people and situations that are encountered. People and new situations are encountered with resistance in the first three chakras. From the Heart chakra, it is acceptance that is characteristic of the way you meet others.

FIFTH CHAKRA: The Throat chakra impels you to express yourself in a creative way. From this center, you view the world as friendly, supportive, and helpful. You feel encouraged to explore your creative potential. You see the world as offering exactly what you need for further growth and awareness. The fifth, sixth, and seventh chakras are transcendent and collective experiences. If you don't act on your creative ideas, someone else will.

SIXTH CHAKRA: The drive to experience ecstasy is the primary need of the Third Eye chakra. Achieving the clear-sightedness that is associated with the Third Eye requires that you collect and synthesize all the divergent aspects of the self and unite them into a single point of awareness. The goal is to develop a point of reflection from which you can witness even your own involvement with life, as it is happening. You impartially observe yourself and others, as you are finally past judgment and comparison. From here, you are detached from the vulnerability of emotional ups and downs.

SEVENTH CHAKRA: By definition, the Crown chakra represents undifferentiated, pure, cosmic energy. When the energy has risen to this level, there is no balanced or unbalanced expression of the energy; it just *is*. This center, which started the process of involution of energy, is the same center that completes the process of evolution. The energy that has been borrowed from the universe to animate individual life is now given back to the universe, and merges personal experience with the collective.

Path

Maintaining a state of balance is a process that requires continual personal adjustment. Everything around you is changing, and to keep up, you must also change by growing and expanding. All of this is part of the process of keeping in harmony. The state of balance for any individual, at any given time, could be called one's path.

The word "path" assumes that there is some place to go, which is misleading. There isn't any place to go; your path is leading you to yourself. You are on your path when you are operating in a state of balance. No two paths are alike. Your path is unique to you even while there are parts shared intimately with others. Every person you come into contact with has a path to follow. With this as an accepted premise, your relationships will operate on a high level, as you can stop judging someone else's choices. At one stage of your path, you may be working with structure and discipline. Strict diet and adherence to daily routine may be what you need. At some point, you may feel rigid from this, and your path changes to one that lets go of structure, thereby maintaining balance in the midst of a seeming lack of form. You have to feel out your own growth, and move in accordance with where you are at the moment, recognizing that others have this same freedom.

The indicator of harmony in your life will be found within you, the individual. You have an inner life and an outer life. Your outer life is your involvement with the social/physical world that surrounds you. Your inner life could be defined as your reaction to that involvement. Harmony exists when your inner and outer lives are in accord with each other. It has to be self-monitored and self-regulated; in other words, the responsibility for maintaining a harmonious existence is completely up to you. This is what makes self-knowledge so important, and sheds light on the ancient axiom: "Seeker, know thyself."

Tao

The Chinese have shown a keen sensitivity for harmonizing with nature. They called this harmonized relationship Tao (pronounced *dow*). This concept is based on the teachings of Lao Tsu recorded in his book, *Tao Te Ching*. There are many definitions of what the Tao means, and all fall short of its simplicity, purity, and depth. Lao Tsu says, "The Tao that can be told is not the eternal Tao." This is reminiscent of what Carlos Castenada is speaking of with the concept of the "Nagual." It is the unnameable, ever-present, and most alive. It is a process that is often analogized to water. Water always moves in the path of least resistance, and when studying the Tao, you are taught to flow, bend, and yield to the environment, as does water. Now the course is checked, now it flows easily, always it is water. If it comes to an obstacle, it goes around it. If it comes to a hole or crevice, it will first fill the hole, then proceed on its course; formless and shapeless, water has no resistance. To study the nature of water is to understand what the Tao is.

Your personal Tao, or "way," represents the course of action that will allow you to be true to your own essential identity and, at the same time, yield to the demands of your environment. Following the Tao creates a feeling of inner peace that is the result of being in tune with the universe; not wondering "what next?", not reflecting on what has been, but simply being relaxed and thoroughly in the moment. Being in harmony creates a feeling of peace. Being out of harmony creates feelings of frustration, anxiety, and tension. These feelings can be read as indications of being off your path. They are the signals alerting you to make an adjustment to re-establish harmony.

Comfort Zone

One of the physical laws of energy is that an imbalanced energy field carries a charge with it. It is said to be ionized, and is considered more volatile than a balanced field. An ionized molecule will bond itself to another molecule to reach a state of balance. The molecule to which it attaches itself must contain just the right energy field to remove the imbalance.

Transferring this model of molecular imbalance to the human situation is perhaps abstract and over-simplified, but it is a helpful means of visualization. Each person has a "comfort zone" which represents his or her state of balance. When you move out of this state you become "charged" and attracted to a life situation that will bring you back to balance. When you are experiencing balance and harmony in your life, you are attracting situations that are within your comfort zone.

At whatever level you may be operating, you seek experiences that keep you within your familiar comfort zone. For example, if you have become accustomed to a particular level of success and start achieving more than that, you will attract a failure to bring you back to your original comfort zone unless you alter your comfort zone level.

While in the unbalanced state, there is a lack of creative choice. The law of attraction binds you to those situations that meet the imbalanced needs. One who is interested in creative choice can easily see the limitations of the charged states. There are alternative techniques given throughout this book for releasing this charged energy. Following the Tao does not remove obstructions from life, but it will help you to pass through them without getting stuck.

Karma

Creating a balance between your inner state of peace and the demands of your environment is your personal challenge, and maintaining the balance by following the Tao is your path. The degree of success you have with this balancing act could be called your karma. Karma can be compared to the axiom of Newtonian physics: "For each and every action, there is an equal and opposite reaction." This principle is described in different ways: "cause and effect," "as ye sow, so shall ye reap," or "you get out of something what you put into it." All are different ways of stating the same principle: the principle of karma.

Karma is a reflection of all that you have put into the universe. Each and every moment you are alive, you are putting energy into the universe by exercising your choices. Each choice you make could be considered an investment in your future. Buddha said, "You are what you think, having become what you thought." The process begins with your thoughts, and follows into action. Your thoughts are powerful programs. You can alter the script of your life by creating a new vision. If you want success and happiness, then you have to stop thinking, "It can't happen to me." Awareness and responsibility for your life are the necessary tools to create personal happiness.

An example of how this principle can be seen is by paying attention to the changes of the energy field created in a relationship. A couple that is skilled in noticing the early signs of tension and is able to deal with it while it's still in its germinating stage has a far greater chance of maintaining a long-term relationship than the couple that avoids the early warning.

Tension is not often dealt with in its earliest forms. Avoidance, without adjustment, leads to a build-up of this energy and not a dispersion of it. When this build-up gets to a critical point, avoidance will not be possible. The release of tension that is then triggered is disproportionate to the situation that set off the release. The shockwave of this much tension being released blows apart many good relationships. The couple that can deal with the tension while it is still in its subtle form is effectively using the model of which we are speaking.

If you want to see a change in your karma, you must recognize that "change" is a verb as well as a noun. To find change you must be willing to initiate it. What kind of changes can be made? Mostly attitudinal ones: Where negativity exists in the intellectual, intuitional, and emotional sphere, it will soon appear in the physical. It takes work to change the attitudes of negativity, but not as much work as it takes to live with the negative results this kind of thinking manifests in your life. The first step in making a change is being aware that it is needed. The second step is to acknowledge that it is possible, and the third step is to understand how to initiate the process.

The principle of karma works on a collective level as well as an individual level. Collective karma is the sum total of all the individual expressions of it. Collective karma attracts social situations that affect everyone, the grossest example being war. World karma is the storehouse, or bank, from which all the individual expressions of it are drawn. In this sense, a person is bound to the potential of the whole.

Changing individual karma to a higher standard, to help create a higher standard of collective karma, is the goal of many practitioners of metaphysics. The first step in improving world karma is to improve the standard of your karma. A balanced energy field will improve the balance of the whole, as this energy is nonreactive and tends to neutralize much of the tension it contacts. It follows that the single most important thing you can do to improve the world situation is to work on bringing balance to your own karma.

Meditation

To balance your energy field and raise your attention to the upper chakras, meditation in all its various forms is required. Meditation is a method of quieting the thinking mind and allowing yourself to fully be in the present moment. This can be achieved through various techniques: walking on the beach and losing yourself in the sunset, yoga, T'ai Chi, creative visualization, focusing on your breath, reciting a mantra, or just sitting.

The goal is the same in all of these forms; to quiet the busy mind and become aware of peace, tranquility, and a sense of oneness with all creation. In meditation, all anxieties, concerns, worries, and ambitions are placed aside. This sounds easy, but it actually takes practice to let go of the many thoughts that continually present themselves. When these thoughts come while you are meditating, simply recognize and dismiss them. You may be surprised at how many things want to be thought of while you are attempting a ten-minute meditation.

Meditation should not be overlooked in your metaphysical pursuits. It has tremendous benefits that you will notice in all aspects of your life. Giving the mind something to do while in meditation can be helpful. In the following meditation, you will be combining your awarenesses of color and the chakras in the exercise.

Color and Chakra Meditation

Plan to spend about fifteen to twenty minutes on this meditation. Sit quietly, close your eyes, and focus on your breath until it becomes regular, with good, deep inhalations and exhalations. With the inbreath, through the nostrils, visualize white light filling the total space of your being. Hold that white light for two to three seconds, then exhale through your mouth. With the exhalation, visualize all the impurities of your body, mind, and spirit leaving in a stream of black light. When you feel totally empty, again breathe deeply through the nostrils, allowing the white light to fill your being, before exhaling the black energy through your mouth. After a few minutes of this breathing exercise, you will be ready to take a color-filled walk up your spine.

Enter the long red carpet of desire. Visualize the light entering from the base of your spine and feel the raw and primal energy. Next, enter the orange room of enthusiasm and courage. Feel the clear orange light revitalize, invigorate, and energize you. Now enter the glow of the yellow vibration. Feel its sharpness stimulate the nervous system, the brain, and intellect. Feel this color around your solar plexus. It is as if you have just turned on light in each of these specific areas.

These first three centers deal with survival (red), security (orange), and intellect (yellow). As you focus upon and send light to these centers, you are healing the etheric body. At this point in the meditation, you should be feeling quite warm.

Now, enter the bright green forest which surrounds the area of your heart. Run through its valleys, hills, and grasses. Allow the energy to heal your love and balance your senses. From green, pass into the hues of blue. Visualize flying through the sky. Receive the blue light of live faith and sweet peace into your being. Float upward into indigo, around the area of your Third

Eye. Feel yourself become receptive to new fields of comprehension and knowledge; feel what it is like to have no boundaries on what you are capable of doing. Feel the lightness of both body and spirit, as you allow yourself to burst into the violet ray at the top of the head: the chamber of the heavenly sphere, the world of the mystic.

Synergy

In 1970, when Buckminster Fuller was lecturing on the college campuses around the United States, he noted that less than 3% of the university staff and students knew of the concept of synergy. His definition of synergy is "behavioral interrelationship of two or more separate components." An operational definition of synergy is: the process of two elements coming together in such a way that what they achieve in their combined form far surpasses what either element could produce independently. There are medical cases where the following example may not be true, but generally the most obvious example of this natural occurrence is the reproductive process. The male and female combine in such a way that they produce something that neither is capable of independently.

Applying this principle to learning theory leads to some interesting possibilities. An analogy might help you better understand how the process of synergy can be applied to learning. Suppose your mind is like an electronic processing computer that is designed to operate on 100 units of energy. Let's suppose that your own body can only generate somewhere between ten and twenty-five units of energy to charge your 100-amp mind. If this were the case, then in an isolated condition, you would only be able to use ten to twenty-five percent of your mind; the approximate amount of the total brain that people are utilizing in everyday life. To use the process of synergy to increase your mind's potential, you would look for other available sources of energy and combine with them.

If thought can be considered a form of energy, accepting the thoughts of others is accomplished by the acceptance of the energy that animated those thoughts. Keep in mind the analogy of the 100-amp mind. If in the process of communicating, two people actually accept each other's thoughts, then, if each had twenty units of mental energy, their combined energy potential would be forty units. This combined capacity far surpasses the individual potential, thus we have synergy.

Sounds easy, but is it? Is it easy to listen fully with the intent of accepting another person's thoughts without defending your own position or thinking about what you are going to say next? The belief in autonomy of thinking and the right of privacy of thought actually make it difficult to either fully share your thoughts or to fully receive the thoughts of others. It is not very ego-satisfying to consider your mind as a tiny transistor in a world-wide thinking machine, but it can be a very useful model in helping you put synergy to work in your life.

The next time you are with others, remember these analogies and see if you can gain some of the energy available through synergy. Consider the other person's thoughts as potential energy for your mind. The more you are fully able to accept the thoughts of those around you, the more energy you will gain. A beneficial side-effect of this exercise will be increased listening skills. Remember, synergy is the process of two organisms coming together. As the component of increased receptivity, you must also be willing to share your thoughts fully.

This theory is actually an extension of the holographic learning theory that is currently being explored by scientists of the mind. In holography, a projected image is split in two by a laser beam, and then reunited by mirrors. This recombined image appears to be three-dimensional as opposed to the conventional method of viewing things in the more limiting two-dimensional way.

Imagine learning how to play the piano by watching someone else play. If this were actually possible, you could learn anything by simply exposing yourself to it. Of course, belief systems would have to be altered for this to take place. If you believe that it would take you five years of practicing piano to become proficient at it, then no amount of exposure will alter that likelihood. Perhaps "genius" is never having heard that you can only learn through years of experience.

This theory does offer a possible explanation for the ability to give a tarot, astrology, or any other type of "reading" to another person. It presupposes that each of us has all potential experiences within ourselves and by exposing oneself to the psyche of another person, the combined images allow the reader to accurately describe the condition of the person's life.

Random Generation of Symbols

After you have worked so diligently on learning the structured use of the disciplines presented in this book, you can now begin to integrate them more casually into everyday use. Every opportunity you have for exercising and sharpening your intuition should be taken advantage of. When the phone rings, who is it? When you are going to meet a new person, what is she like? When something unexpected happens, what is the meaning of the event?

To facilitate this you can use methods for randomly generating the symbols of metaphysics. These are all "quickie" types of readings that are not used for deeper insights but are effective for sharpening your intuition.

TAROT: Keep a deck of Tarot cards readily accessible in your home. When the telephone rings, cut the cards and ask yourself, who is it and what is the message? Another quickie is to fan the cards on the table and draw one on any given situation. Drawing one card from the deck to represent a general theme for the day is yet another method.

PALMISTRY: Notice where you are getting cuts and hurts on your hands. You can use the symbols of palmistry to connect the afflicted area in your hand to an aspect of your life that needs more attention.

NUMEROLOGY: There are numerous occasions during the day when numbers randomly pop up before you. Each of these times is an opportunity to sharpen your intuition. Notice the number of your parking stall, keep it in mind as a clue to the theme of what you will experience after parking the car. Addresses, ticket stub numbers, telephone numbers, and license plate numbers are all opportunities to use numerology in daily life.

ASTROLOGY: Notice the types of people you are attracting into your life. Is there a dominant sign represented? Often this is symbolic of a part of your birth chart that you are working on.

The *Sabian Symbols* is a book that symbolically represents each one of the 360 degrees of the zodiac. Dane Rudhyar and Marc Edmund Jones have provided the most popular sources, though there are several others in print. Permanent symbols relevant to timing can be found by looking up the degrees of your progressed planets. The degrees of important transits can be another use of the Sabian symbols. Random symbols can be generated by opening the book to any page, and reading the symbol that your finger points to.

I CHING: The method of opening the book at random and pointing to a line for a spontaneous reading works exceptionally well. This method also works with the *Bible* and other books of wisdom.

EVENTS: Once you have sharpened your intuition to the point that you can see the meaning of seemingly unrelated events, then all of life becomes symbolic. An example is when you are working in the kitchen and accidently cut your finger. It is often revealing to analyze what you were thinking about at the moment you cut yourself. Were you thinking cutting thoughts about someone? There are myriad clues throughout the day that can show you both the power of your thoughts and how interconnected the world really is.

When you have extended your intuition to include the events of life as a source of symbols, you will never be without the tools of the trade. When you first begin on this path, the cards, coins, and planets are necessary tools. These sharpen and strengthen your primary tool: intuition. Now that you have opened this door, all of life is available for reading.

Index